THE BOOK OF JUDGES

The Book of Judges has typically been treated either as a historical account of the period between the conquest of Israel and the rise of the monarchy, or as an ancient Israelite work of literary fiction.

In this new approach to a book which has become the focus of significant scholarly attention in recent years, Marc Zvi Brettler contends that Judges is essentially a political tract which argues for the legitimacy of Davidic kingship.

The book contains a variety of diverse stories, and Brettler analyzes a cross-section of these to support his case. Theoretical discussion of the genres employed is combined with an overview of the ways in which the book has conventionally been treated.

The purposes behind several paradigmatic passages, such as the Ehud story, the Barak–Deborah story and poem and the long Samson cycle are considered, and the functions of the book's introduction, and its horrific ending, are given particular attention.

The Book of Judges skilfully and accessibly shows the tension between the stories in their original forms, and how they were altered and re-used to create a book with a very different meaning. It will be important reading for all those studying this part of the Bible and those interested in the editing of biblical texts.

Marc Zvi Brettler is Dora Golding Professor of Biblical Studies and Chair of the Department of Near Eastern and Judaic Studies, Brandeis University, Massachussetts, USA. He is the author of *The Creation of History in Ancient Israel*, also published by Routledge, and co-author of *The New Oxford Annotated Bible*.

OLD TESTAMENT READINGS
Series Editor: Keith Whitelam
University of Stirling, UK

THE BOOK OF JUDGES
Marc Zvi Brettler

GENESIS
Mark G. Brett

EZRA–NEHEMIAH
Lester L. Grabbe

PSALMS
Alastair G. Hunter

THE BOOK OF JUDGES

Marc Zvi Brettler

London and New York

First published 2002
by Routledge
11 New Fetter Lane, London EC4P 4EE

Simultaneously published in the USA and Canada
by Routledge
29 West 35th Street, New York, NY 10001

Routledge is an imprint of the Taylor & Francis Group

Typeset in Great Britain by Saxon Graphics Ltd, Derby
Printed and bound in Great Britain by TJ International Ltd,
Padstow, Cornwall

British Library Cataloging in Publication Data
A catalogue record for this book is available from the British Library

Library of Congress Cataloging in Publication Data
Brettler, Marc Zvi.
The Book of Judges/Marc Zvi Brettler.
p. cm – (Old Testament readings)
Includes bibliographical references and index.
1. Bible. O.T. Judges–Criticism, interpretation, etc. I. Title. II. Series.
BS1305.2 .B74 2001
222'.3206–dc21   2001019667
ISBN 0-415-16216-5 (hbk.)
ISBN 0-415-16217-3 (pbk.)

TO TALYA,
WHO HAS TAUGHT ME SO MUCH
OVER THE LAST FIFTEEN YEARS.

CONTENTS

PREFACE

Judges has become a "hot" book. This was not the case several decades ago, when it was seen as sandwiched between the much more significant Torah (Pentateuch) and the more theologically relevant prophetic corpus. But tastes have changed. The so-called historical texts, whether as the second section of the Christian Bibles, or as the first part of the second section of Jewish Bibles ("former prophets"), have been the focus of intense interest in the last two decades. Part of this is the result of the growing literary study of biblical texts. Books such as Judges and Samuel are now appreciated for their literary technique and merit. In addition, the Copenhagen school, with Niels Peter Lemche and Thomas Thompson at their core, have continued to raise very fundamental questions about the historicity of all biblical texts, and have brought this issue into both the scholarly and popular spotlight. This has raised the question that is the focus of much of this book: If Judges is not history, what is it?

The noted classical historian, Elias Bickerman, wrote a study of Jonah, Daniel, Ecclesiastes and Esther, which he called *Four Strange Books of the Bible* (Bickerman 1967). Had I written that book, Judges would have been included as well. It is strange on so many levels. Joshua dies twice in the book (1:1; 2:8). Many of the "judges" are really anti-heroic – think of Samson and his womanizing, Jephthah and his vow, Gideon and his lack of faith. There is a strange mixing of genres in the book: most of the stories are relatively long, and focus on a single individual ("major judges"), but at two points we find judges noted in little more than lists (10:1–4; 12:8–15), with such fascinating information as (10:4) "He had thirty sons, who rode on thirty burros and owned thirty boroughs in the region of Gilead."[1] Women are unusually prominent throughout the book, and play a wide range of roles in it. And some of the stories are quite fantastic – how are we to take a narrative which suggests that a woman was butchered into twelve parts, and each one was sent to a tribe of Israel (19:29)?

These are the types of questions that will be the focus of the rest of this study. I begin by showing how and why the old approach to Judges, which saw the book as a source for ancient Israelite history, has disappeared from the scholarly world. This is followed by a discussion of traditional literary approaches to biblical texts, and a suggestion that a new type of literary–historical approach must be developed to study books like Judges. The rest of the book attempts to develop and illustrate this approach.

The core of the book examines several of the stories incorporated in Judges. We begin by comparing the Ehud, Othniel and Shamgar stories which highlight the diverse sources incorporated in Judges. This is followed by a study of the longest cycle of stories in Judges, the Samson material. This material is extremely rich, and especially because it is composed of a collection of stories, a careful study of it will raise several issues relevant to understanding how the book as a whole might function. Judges 4–5, the prose and poetic narratives concerning Deborah, offer a rare opportunity to explore the different underpinnings of prose and poetic historiography, and how they might be related.

The book of Judges does not in its entirety deal with judges. The first one and a half chapters of the book concern the transition from the period of Joshua to the period of the judges, and the final five chapters, often considered an appendix to the book, contain two stories in which judges play no role. One chapter of this work will be dedicated to studying some of the features of the concluding and introductory chapters of the book. These lead directly to the final chapter, which will examine the nature of Judges as a book – seeing whether or not the whole is greater than the sum of its parts.

It is impossible in a work of this sort to explain every passage in Judges – that is the job of a commentary, not an introductory work in the Old Testament Readings series. This book is not intended as a commentary: instead its focus, following the series' name, is on "reading" – how are we to read both the individual stories and the book as a whole? Though not all stories will be covered, I hope those examined may function paradigmatically. What did they mean, and why were they written and preserved? Why were they collected together into a book? Is this a loose collection, in which case the book should not be taken too seriously as a whole, or is it a heavily edited work, with a unified theme? These are the types of questions which will be brought to bear in the following chapters.

My interest in Judges goes back to my graduate student days, when, close to twenty years ago, I took a doctoral exam on the Book of Judges. There was little secondary literature then on the book, and I completed the exam with more questions than answers. The current book thus represents several decades of thinking about these questions and teaching Judges.

I would like to thank my examiners from two decades ago, Michael Fishbane, Nahum Sarna, and the late Marvin Fox for encouraging me to further explore some very tentative observations made about the book by a very young graduate student. Much more recently, I appreciate the help that my research assistant, Sarah Shectman, offered me in various stages of preparing the manuscript and in proofreading. Alan Lenzi, also a graduate student at Brandeis, compiled the indices. Professor Everett Fox read the proofs the book, and called many errors to my attention. The series editor, Keith Whitelam, and the Routledge editor, Richard Stoneman, offered much helpful advice, especially in the book's early stages. My family, Monica, Talya and Ezra, were understanding when the summer of 2000 was spent with Judges rather than at the beach – I never could have completed this without their support. It is with great joy and pride that I dedicate this book to my בכורה, my eldest daughter, Talya.

ABBREVIATIONS

AB   Anchor Bible
ABD   *Anchor Bible Dictionary*. Edited by D.N. Freedman. 6
            vols. New York, 1992.
AnBib   Analecta Biblica
BBB   Bonner biblische Beiträge
BBET   Beiträge zur biblischen Exegese und Theologie
Bib   *Biblica*
BibInt   *Biblical Interpretation*
BJRL   *Bulletin of the John Rylands University Library of
            Manchester*
BJS   Brown Judaic Studies
BN   *Biblische Notizen*
BTB   *Biblical Theology Bulletin*
BZAW   Beihefte zur Zeitschrift für die alttestamentliche
            Wissenschaft
CBC   Cambridge Bible Commentary
CBQ   *Catholic Biblical Quarterly*
DJD   Discoveries in the Judaean Desert
ErIsr   *Eretz Israel*
GKC   *Gesenius' Hebrew Grammar*. Edited by E. Kautzsch.
            Translated by A.E. Cowley. 2nd edition. Oxford, 1910.
HALOT   Koehler, L., W. Baumgartner, and J.J. Stamm, *The
            Hebrew and Aramaic Lexicon of the Old Testament*.
            Translated under the supervision of M.E. Richardson. 4
            vols. Leiden, 1994–9.
HAR   *Hebrew Annual Review*
HSS   Harvard Semitic Studies
HTR   *Harvard Theological Review*
HUCA   *Hebrew Union College Annual*
ICC   International Critical Commentary

Int	*Interpretation*
JAAR	*Journal of the American Academy of Religion*
JANESCU	*Journal of the Ancient Near Eastern Society of Columbia University*
JBL	*Journal of Biblical Literature*
JNES	*Journal of Near Eastern Studies*
JQR	*Jewish Quarterly Review*
JR	*Journal of Religion*
JSOT	*Journal for the Study of the Old Testament*
JSOTSup	Journal for the Study of the Old Testament: Supplement Series
NCB	New Century Bible
NJPS	New Jewish Publication Society Bible translation
NLH	*New Literary History*
OBT	Overtures to Biblical Theology
RevQ	*Revue de Qumran*
SBL	Society of Biblical Literature
SBT	Studies in Biblical Theology
ScrHier	Scripta Hierosolymitana
Sem	*Semitica*
SHANE	Studies in the History of the Ancient Near East
SWBAS	Social World of Biblical Antiquity Series
TZ	*Theologische Zeitschrift*
VT	*Vetus Testamentum*
VTSup	Supplements to Vetus Testamentum
YNER	Yale Near Eastern Researches
ZAH	*Zeitschrift fürAlthebräistik*
ZAW	*Zeitschrift für die alttestamentliche Wissenschaft*

Biblical books (following the conventions of *JBL*):

Gen	Genesis
Exod	Exodus
Lev	Leviticus
Num	Numbers
Deut	Deuteronomy
Josh	Joshua
Judg	Judges
1–2 Sam	1–2 Samuel
1–2 Kgs	1–2 Kings
Isa	Isaiah
Jer	Jeremiah

Ezek	Ezekiel
Hos	Hosea
Joel	Joel
Amos	Amos
Obad	Obadiah
Jonah	Jonah
Mic	Micah
Nah	Nahum
Hab	Habakkuk
Zeph	Zephaniah
Hag	Haggai
Zech	Zechariah
Mal	Malachi
Ps	Psalms
Job	Job
Prov	Proverbs
Ruth	Ruth
Cant	Canticles (Song of Songs)
Qoh	Qohelet (Ecclesiastes)
Lam	Lamentations
Esth	Esther
Dan	Daniel
Ezra	Ezra
Neh	Nehemiah
1–2 Chr	1–2 Chronicles

Note: Most abbreviations follow *The SBL Handbook of Style for Ancient Near Eastern, Biblical, and Early Christian Studies*, ed. P. H. Alexander *et al.* (Peabody, MA, 1999).

1

JUDGES AND
THE HISTORIAN

As readers of the text, it matters whether or not Judges should be
viewed as history in the sense of a work attempting to convey the
real past. If we believe that the biblical authors subscribed to the
famous words of Lucian in *How to Write History*: "The historian's
one task is to tell it as it happened" (*apud* Wiseman 1993: 122), we
would conclude that the main goal of the material collected in
Judges was to reflect what happened in the pre-monarchic period.
We would then ask the following central question: Is it an accurate
depiction of the past?

However, if we do not believe that the main goal of these texts'
authors was to depict the past, we will judge these texts differently, and we would ask different questions of them. Our primary
questions would *not* be: Were the authors good historians? Or:
Given that all history involves the narrative reworking of events,
how accurately did this particular set of narrative reworkings of the
past capture the real past? Instead, we would need to ask a fundamentally different set of questions. These would include: Is the
real past of the pre-monarchic period reflected at all in these texts?
To what extent do they only reflect the period of their authors?
Finally, if the goal of the authors was not to recreate the past, was
not motivated by "antiquarian interest" (Halpern 1988; Brettler
1990a), we must ask: What was the author of each story (and the
book as a whole) trying to accomplish?

Determining the nature, or genre, of Judges, and thus deciding
which questions we should be asking, is a difficult task. Elsewhere
I have offered a broad definition of a historical text as "a narrative
that presents a past" (Brettler 1995). Judges fits this definition, but
that is not very helpful in determining which set of questions noted
above should be used for exploring it. Much more decisive is
whether it is a historical text in the sense of a narrative that presents

(or is attempting to present) *the* past, in other words, if it is written as history of the sort now found in books such as *The Cambridge History of Judaism* or *The Cambridge Ancient History*, whose authors are expected to do their best at letting us know what really happened, or if its goal is altogether different.

This problem is compounded by the fact that there is no form-critical marker in any biblical text that says: "I am a text that is attempting to accurately depict the past." Matitiahu Tsevat expresses this succinctly by noting that from the perspective of the self-presentation of the biblical texts, "the waters of Noah are no less real than the waters of Shiloah" (Tsevat 1980: 184). The lack of a match between the historicity of a text and its form comes through clearly in a cursory examination of biblical genealogies. Though scholars might debate which genealogies accurately reflect real father–son relationships, most, if not all scholars would agree that some genealogies, especially those preserved in some of the lists in books like Ezra–Nehemiah, should be read in a straightforward fashion as B was the real son of A. On the other hand, genealogies which have exactly the same form and structure should sometimes be read "metaphorically to express other social relationships where real kinship is not involved" (R.R. Wilson 1992: 930; 1977). Yet other genealogies are believed to be forgeries, in which the author, for ideological reasons, attempts to create real kinship relationships that never existed. The genealogy of Zadok in 1 Chr 5:34, "proving" that the reigning family of priests was actually descended from Levi, or the genealogy of Caleb in 1 Chr 2:18, "proving" that his (Kenizzite!) family belonged to Judah, are parade examples of this phenomenon. However, these three types of genealogies, the real, the metaphorical, and the falsified, all look the same. To restate this crucial point: There is no such thing as text which is form-critically marked as true or historical.

This point is not adequately recognized in biblical studies, which is often practiced in a highly charged theological atmosphere. Comparable observations, however, have been made in classical studies. For example, in a recent study "Truth and Untruth in Herodotus and Thucydides," J.L. Moles observes that there are three explanations for why ancient historians sometimes do not tell the truth: "error, dishonesty, or misconception of history's true function" (Moles 1993: 90). The same is true of the ancient authors of Israelite history whose works became incorporated into the Bible.

The fact that there is no fundamental marker for accurate historical texts explains much of the debate that has raged in recent years concerning the historicity of particular biblical texts. The texts themselves are not "marked" in terms of their reliability. In addition, the dating of the texts, and thus their distance from the events they describe, is often uncertain; we have little sense of who wrote the biblical texts, and therefore what the authors' goals or interests might have been. Furthermore, external evidence that can either confirm or disconfirm these texts is lacking, due in large part to the fact that very few ancient Israelite documents have survived from antiquity, most likely because they were written on parchment, which deteriorated. Archaeology can only help on the periphery or in very broad areas, such as suggesting that Joshua may not be read as straightforward "actual" history (Dever 1990: 37–84). Thus, it is typically internal analysis, which is recognized as quite subjective, that suggests how a biblical historical text should be read.

The twentieth century, especially in its last two decades, has seen a remarkable change in the way that Judges has been evaluated as a historical text. For much of the century, it was taken by most scholars as a somewhat embellished account of what happened between the period of the conquest and the rise of the monarchy. This goes back to earlier attitudes from the beginning of critical biblical scholarship. For example, in Julius Wellhausen's 1881 *Encyclopedia Britannica* article "Israel" (Wellhausen 1973), the book of Judges is largely paraphrased. The judges within the book are taken as historical figures, the stories are understood to be organized in chronological order, and the numbers in the text are seen as accurate.

This tendency to paraphrase biblical accounts continues with many of the major histories of Israel. It is most obvious in Bright, one of the more conservative historians. He speaks with certainty of "the period of Judges." He takes the text at face value, keeps the biblical chronology, and even notes, "We can add very little to what the Bible tells us of the various leaders, called judges..." (Bright 1981: 177–81). Even Martin Noth, who is often contrasted with Bright, takes most of the stories at face value, and offers a paraphrase of them in his *History* (Noth 1960). Noth is more willing than Bright to rearrange the chronological order of the stories, and he does not paraphrase them all,[1] but his basic starting point seems to be that they provide reliable information for the modern historian who wants to reconstruct the history of pre-monarchic Israel.

A detailed examination of a study by Abraham Malamat from 1954 reflects the attitude that prevailed through the middle of the twentieth century, and the problems of this approach. Malamat wrote on the very difficult episode preserved in Judg 3:7–11, concerning the defeat by Othniel of King Cushan-rishathaim of Aram-naharaim (Malamat 1954: 231–42). While Malamat notes that the material in Judges is sometimes schematic, he assumes that it is reliable. He recognizes that the king's name, Cushan-rishathaim, which means "the dark double-wicked one," is problematic, but he assumes that it is the corruption of some other name, specifically that Irsu was corrupted to Rishathaim. Even though Othniel is from the south, Malamat takes at face value the text's comment that Cushan-rishathaim was from Aram-naharaim, the area of modern Syria, and assumes that this invasion from the North occurred at a time of documented Egyptian weakness. In his concluding paragraph, he notes:

> The situation in the north makes it clear not only that it is unreasonable to doubt the existence of a Cushan Rishathaim but that the constellation of political forces in this area even renders plausible the rise and expansion of a king in Aram Naharaim.
>
> (Malamat 1954: 242)

This argument is full of problems. Malamat never asks what the likely genre of this short text in Judges is – he automatically assumes that its author is attempting to convey what really happened. Had his ear been more attuned to the absurdity of the name of Cushan-rishathaim – "the dark double-wicked one" – and the fact that it even rhymes with Aram-naharaim, he might not have been so quick to assume that this text is attempting to narrate *the* past. Furthermore, he sidesteps the geographical problems involved in having a southern judge attack a northern king; this account is like saying that Mexico fought the United States, and the army from North Dakota defended it![2] Finally, Malamat does not probe the implications of the fact that the Israelite hero "just happens" to already be known from Josh 15:17 and its parallel in Judg 1:13.

In all fairness to Malamat, it is only since the work of Richter in 1964 that we have a better understanding of what stands behind Judg 3:7–11 (Richter 1964: 23–6). It is now generally agreed that these verses are a composition offering a paradigm of *the* positive judge. This explains why Othniel is known from elsewhere – the historian "borrowed" a known figure, and composed something new about him. It also explains why he defeats "dark double wickedness" – this is logical for a paradigm, though highly unlikely in real life. Finally, in a paradigm, geography does not really matter.

This particular aspect of Richter's theory about the composition of Judges has won wide acceptance for the simple reason that it explains the odd features of this text, and fits it well within the book, as the first story of a (major) judge. All explanations must justify why particular biblical texts were created or preserved – it succeeds in a much less forced fashion than Malamat's suggestion. Malamat's proposal is not absolutely impossible – it cannot be disproved. But its starting point – that the Bible is historically correct unless some unequivocal piece of evidence indicates otherwise, and thus plausibility implies probability – is methodologically problematic for biblical history, as it is for any historical reconstruction.[3] We now recognize that this starting point inevitably leads to circular logic – somehow, somewhere, some sort of "confirmation" of the text's history is discovered.

By the 1970s, the type of methodology used by Malamat was beginning to be called into question. In *The Early History of Israel*, the great French scholar Roland de Vaux notes that the "age of judges" is an artificial construct, and he is skeptical of the veracity of many of these stories, which were written much later than the events they describe (de Vaux 1978: 751–63).

A History of Ancient Israel and Judah, published in 1986 by Miller and Hayes, follows in the footsteps of de Vaux. It is a significant new type of history, which is often much more methodologically explicit than its predecessors about the problems of the Bible as a source, and in many ways it is symbolic of, and helped to further precipitate the "crisis" of using the Bible as a straightforward historical source.[4] Like de Vaux, Miller and Hayes are not comfortable with the typical designation of this period, and speak instead of "what is often called 'the period of the Judges'" (Miller and Hayes 1986: 87). They note that the stories are often schematic or typological, and "can hardly be accepted at face value for purposes of historical reconstruction" (Miller and Hayes 1986: 87), though they tentatively put more confidence in particular stories, and ultimately end up offering paraphrases of some of them. Even the typically iconoclastic Gösta W. Ahlström paraphrases many of the stories in his history, though unlike Bright he tries to bring external evidence to bear. For example, Ahlström finds the story where Ehud confronts Eglon the Moabite king problematic, since there is no evidence for Moabites in this period (Ahlström 1993: 377).

In sum, most historians of Israel now recognize the problematic nature of Judges as a source for ancient Israelite history. This realization stands in the way of their desire to fill in the history, which results in a strange tension: They claim that Judges is problematic as a source, but continue to paraphrase at least certain sections of it. Had they been more fair to their methodological considerations, they might have left this period blank, or used archeological material and analogies concerning pre-monarchic organization from other societies to fill in the picture (Frick 1985; Hackett 1998), ignoring the evidence found in Judges.

The most articulate, carefully reasoned expression of the problem of using Judges as a straightforward narrative recounting the past comes from approximately the same time as Miller and Hayes' history, by the Copenhagen scholar Niels Peter Lemche in his *Early Israel*. Based on his analysis of oral literature and careful investigation of how traditions grow, especially in the pre-literary stage, he notes:

> This means that the nature of the sources dealing with the period of the Judges prevent [*sic*] our being able to write a history of this period. We cannot even permit ourselves to use the various traditions of the Judges as historical references to individual events which actually occurred during the premonarchic period.
>
> (Lemche 1985: 379)

He expresses quite clearly what this would imply for the Ehud narrative:

> ... we should ignore the details, including such names as Ehud and Eglon, or even, for that matter, Israel and Moab. Thus we would no longer automatically be able to assign a particular milieu to this narrative of the period of the Judges. It might just as easily be pre-Israelite, but assimilated into Israelite tradition. It might just as easily derive from the period of the monarchy, although the oral tradition has assigned it to the period of the Judges. In short, we have no way whatsoever, to determine whether any historical tradition at all underlies the narrative in Jdg 3,12–30, as long as we lack other sources. Precisely the

same judgment applies to most of the other traditions in
the Book of Judges.

(Lemche 1985: 383)

Once stated so clearly, and put into the broader perspective of
how traditions develop, this position is quite obvious, and it is not
surprising that it has gained general assent.

My belief in the correctness of Lemche's position concerning the
period of the judges does not mean that I agree with the more
recent studies completed by Lemche and his Copenhagen col-
league, Thomas L. Thompson (Lemche 1998; Thompson 1999).
These scholars have raised extreme skepticism concerning almost
all biblical traditions, and have suggested that much of the Hebrew
Bible is a late post-exilic, Hellenistic creation. This is not the place
to fully debate this broader issue,[5] since I concede their argument
concerning the (lack of) historicity for Judges. I would just note
that had I been writing on Kings, the types of questions I would
be asking would be different, because unlike Judges, (1) *sections*
of Kings were written relatively close to the events they narrate;
and (2) it is likely that *some* archival material is preserved in Kings.

Nor should my agreement with Lemche suggest a still broader
agreement with certain historians and philosophers of history who
are deeply skeptical about the ability of narrative history to reflect
the real past. I do not believe that either as a result of Hayden
White's studies of historical discourse, or the literary currents of
deconstructionism or post-modernism, we must speak of the end
of history as a discipline (Iggers 1997: 118–40). Various scholars
have pointed out that the well-known critique of objectivity in
Peter Novick's *That Noble Dream* is really quite overstated, and in
any case, has not stopped him from trying to write history (Novick
1988; Haskell 1998: 145–73).

As I have outlined in *The Creation of History in Ancient Israel*
(1995), I am more sympathetic to more specific claims made about
ancient historians, specifically that they rarely partake in the perceived Rankean ideal of telling it as it really was, which developed
only with the rise of professional university historians in the last
few centuries. I would add to the scholars cited there the observations from G.W. Bowersock's influential *Fiction as History: Nero to
Julian*, who notes that in antiquity there was "a general indiffer-
ence to the distinction between history and myth" and "the overt
creation of fiction as a means of rewriting or even inventing the

past was a serious business for many of the ancients" (Bowersock 1994: 9, 12–13). Entertainment was also an important part of ancient historical writing (Wiseman 1993: 139–40). Sometimes the point that needed to be illustrated or the moral that needed to be told was too important to be reined in by facts (Moles 1993: 120). These observations are as true of Judges as they are of the classical works that Bowersock and others have explored. This would suggest that Judges should not be studied to reconstruct ancient Israelite history of the pre-monarchic period. Nor should we examine it as a historical work by asking how it recreates the past that it is purporting to narrate, since (1) we have no independent method to create that past; and more significantly (2) its main objective was not recreating the past. Our study must find a different point of entry into the book.

2

READING JUDGES AS LITERATURE?

If we are not going to approach Judges as history, it seems that we should study it as literature.[1] This contrast between history and literature is well-entrenched in biblical studies, predominantly thanks to John van Seters' *In Search of History* (van Seters 1975b: 1), which called attention to Johan Huizinga's essay "A Definition of the Concept of History." Huizinga claims that: "The sharp distinction between history and literature lies in the fact that the former is almost entirely lacking in that element of play which underlies literature from beginning to end" (Huizinga 1975: 6). Many scholars would now claim his contrast is too sharp, though it continues to influence the field.[2]

To anticipate my conclusions, I would suggest that this dichotomy is false. Moreover, as I have argued elsewhere, it is often misleading to call the Bible literature (Brettler 1995: 14–17). It is anachronistic, and often suggests inappropriately that the Bible is "Literature." Given the great diversity of sources of different literary merit, including lists and genealogies, this appellation for the collection as a whole is clearly problematic. I am deeply sympathetic to a point made by Robert P. Carroll, that reading the Bible as literature is a "misreading of the text" (Carroll 1993: 89).[3]

Since texts from Judges will be the focus of this study, it is best to commence exploring the literary nature of biblical historical texts by looking at historical texts outside of Judges; these will raise certain problems and possibilities that will be helpful for exploring Judges. I begin with the treatment of the Tower of Babel story (Gen 11:1–9) in J.P. Fokkelman's *Narrative Art in Genesis* (Fokkelman 1975). I treat the material in Genesis 11 as "historical" in the sense noted in the previous chapter as "a narrative that presents a past." While Fokkelman's book is a quarter of a century old, it offers a proper starting place for several reasons. First of all, as (one of) the first synthetic books of its type, it is very self-conscious of its premises, and articulates them in a particularly clear way. Additionally, the manner in which it sees structure as a, or possibly the, central interpretive key has become standard for many biblical scholars, and is worthy of serious re-examination. This book played a very central role in the "paradigm shifts" of biblical studies in the last few decades, coming at a time when the historical nature of the Genesis narratives, defended so forcefully by Albright, Gordon, Speiser and others (Speiser 1964: xxxvii–lii), was just beginning to be questioned by John van Seters and Thomas Thompson (van Seters 1975a; Thompson 1974). Fokkelman continues to be a productive scholar (Fokkelman 1999), whose positions have not shifted greatly since he produced his seminal work.

Many of Fokkelman's claims were quite revolutionary in 1975, particularly his question, "But is diachronic research really necessary to the interpretation of texts?" (Fokkelman 1975: 2). He further suggests:

> If to the creators of the prose of the so-called historical books of the Old Testament it was of fundamental importance to express themselves in narrative art ... then for the interpretation of the texts it is equally fundamental to understand these texts as literary creations and to recognize their modes of existence as linguistic works of art.
>
> (Fokkelman 1975: 5)

He observes: "We may say, in other words ..., that the stories from Genesis have the ontological status of the literary work of art" (Fokkelman 1975: 6). Within a scholarly world concerned primarily with questions of history and history of religion, where source- and form-criticism were the major scholarly tools, these were huge, breathtaking claims, which along with similar arguments by others,[4] helped to change in the most fundamental way the manner in which the Bible was read in the academy.

A central claim of Fokkelman is that stories gain meaning through their structure. For example, in his presentation of the Tower of Babel pericope, he offers the following diagram:

A The entire land ... one language (v. 1)
   B There (v. 2)
      C One to another (v. 3)
         D Come on! Let's make bricks (v. 3)
            E Let's build for ourselves (v. 4)
               F A city and a tower (v. 4)
                     X The LORD descended to see (v. 5)
               F' The city and the tower (v. 5)
            E' Which the people had built (v. 5)
         D' Come on! Let's confound (v. 7)
      C' One the language of the other (v. 7)
   B' From there (v. 8)
A' The language of the entire land (v. 9)

                                       (Fokkelman 1975: 22)[5]

Two questions must be asked about this diagram: (1) Is the structure really there? (2) Is this structure artistic, literary or otherwise?

The first question is really the most fundamental one: How are we to know when a structure discerned by a modern scholar for an ancient biblical text is correct? Few cases are as certain as Gen 9:6, which has a clear chiastic (ABCCBA) structure (Klaus 1999): "Whoever sheds the blood of a human, because he is a human his blood shall be shed." However, Gen 11:1–9 is much more ambiguous. It is true that the unit is framed by the words "the entire land," forming what many would call an inclusio or envelope figure (Watson 1986: 282–7). However, given that the same phrase appears also in vv. 4 and 8, is it legitimate to single out their uses only in vv. 1 and 9, or would their appearance in vv. 4 and 8 have interfered with the creation of, or perception of, the concentric symmetry?[6] Similarly, both B and B' share the word "there" – but what of the use of the same word in vv. 7 and 9? Is a single common word sufficient to create a parallelism, especially when it is repeated elsewhere in the unit? Is it legitimate to just skip v. 6 in this analysis? Is it permissible that D, E, and F are all from two consecutive verses, while D', E' and F' are spread out among several verses, or would this negate the proposed chiastic structure? The most general questions are: To what extent must X and X' be parallel for us to see a structure? What happens if X and X' are of different sizes? Need the parallels be exact, or may they be, as is often proposed by others, thematic? May we use particular occurrences of a common word in a pericope to create parallelisms, even if the word is found in other places in the unit? To repeat the critique of James Kugel on a different part of Fokkelman's book: "True enough, his diagram is symmetrical – but is the text?" (Kugel

1981b: 225). Too often scholars are creating, rather than seeing, a structure (Boda 1996: 55–70). To adapt Samuel Sandmel's neologism of "parallelomaniacs," such structures are too often the products of chiasmaniacs (Boda 1996: 55–70; Butterworth 1992: 18–61).

Even in cases where the text has some sort of structure, it is not clear that this makes the text "literary" or "literature." It is possible, especially in an oral culture, that "true" chiastic structuring was used by the authors/tellers/reciters/singer to organize their thoughts, and that the audience expected it as a matter of formal structure, just as we expect a "sincerely" or a "yours truly" near the end of a letter. Chiasm might then be a formal structure, much like the B part of the poetic verse was understood in the pre-Kugel and Alter era, as a *formal* seconding of the A part, which typically adds little meaning to it, simply parroting what preceded (Gevirtz 1973; Watson 1986: 114–59; Kugel 1981a; Alter 1985). It is not correct to presume that a device like a chiasm is aesthetic, rather than formally compositional, a trope rather than a schema.[7]

Additionally, studies by Fokkelman and others are incorrect for presenting a model where structure is the only, or even the main determinant of meaning. To state the obvious: We would read this story about the tower of Babel differently if it were written by a pre-exilic Judean, an exilic Jew in Babylon between 586 and 539, or a Babylonian-Persian Jew after the conquest of Cyrus, even if the structure of the story did not change one iota. But this does not come through at all from Fokkelman's reading, where structure and word-choice – intrinsic features of the biblical text – determine the story's meaning, to the total exclusion of extrinsic features such as the historical situation which might have influenced its production.

More than any other historical book, Samuel, especially First Samuel, has been the subject of book-length studies, which from their titles and/or contents need to be considered literary in nature. These include Peter Miscall's *1 Samuel: A Literary Reading* (Miscall 1986), Moshe Garsiel's *The First Book of Samuel: A Literary Study of Comparative Structures, Analogies and Parallels* (Garsiel 1985), J. P. Fokkelman's *Narrative Art and Poetry in the Books of Samuel* (Fokkelman 1981–93), and Robert Polzin's *Samuel and the Deuteronomist* (Polzin 1989). My second extended example comes from Robert Polzin's chapter "Providential Delays," in his *Samuel and the Deuteronomist* (Polzin 1989). This chapter focuses on 1 Samuel 24–26, which narrate the flight of David from Saul. Chapter 24 narrates David's flight to Ein-Gedi, where he had the opportunity to kill Saul while Saul was going to the bathroom in the very same cave where David and his men were hiding; chapter 25 tells how David confronted Nabal and ended up marrying Abigail; chapter 26 narrates David's flight to Ziph, where he could have killed the sleeping Saul, but did not. Each of these units reads quite well independently of the others. The commonalties shared by chapters 24 and 26 are particularly striking, especially the way in which David in both chapters rebukes his men for even thinking of laying a hand on "the Lord's anointed" – an expression which typifies these chapters.[8] Yet, chapter 26 does not suggest that it recognizes chapter 24, nor does it reflect any awareness of the fact that it is a repeat of what had just happened! It is thus not surprising that most *critical* scholars see these chapters as originally independent units which were edited together (McCarter 1980: 386–7).

Polzin introduces his chapter "Providential Delays" with the following:

> Nothing excites a biblicist's historical impulses more than a series of parallel episodes strung out along the storyline like a string of pearls. If "these chapters (24, 25, 26) show David being saved from himself, or rather from the consequences of deeds potentially disastrous to his own interests," and if in all three chapters "David refrains from violence against an enemy," then indeed, such repetition inclines many interpreters to fond thoughts of redaction. It is to be expected, then, that Klaus Koch in a classic form-critical work gives prominence to 1 Samuel 24 and 26 by placing them second (after Gen. 12, 20, 26) in his series of analyses of duplicated stories. Certainly like that earlier triple variation on the theme of the ancestor of Israel in danger, not just chapters 24 and 26, but all three episodes in chapters 24, 25, and 26 can be viewed as redaction-related variations on David's success in avoiding any action that would later jeopardize the integrity of his rule. But what if I foolishly refuse to hand over the fruits of my interpretive labors to anonymous redactors who, as Nabal would say, "come from I do not know where"? And what if the story of David's sparing Saul's life comprise a narrative unit that, like Abigail herself, has discretion and good judgment, quite apart from any literary-historical considerations one might entertain?
>
> (Polzin 1989: 205)

Polzin typifies biblical scholars in suggesting that we must either study the parts, *or* the whole – this is an either/or proposition. In contrast, in one of the early articles advocating what has since become known as "the literary approach," Bernhard Anderson suggests:

> If I am not mistaken, a new generation of biblical scholars has arisen that wants to move beyond this kind of analysis [by which he meant source- and form-criticism] to some sort of synthesis, beyond a method that is rigidly diachronic to one that gives appropriate weight to the synchronic dimension of the text.
>
> (B. Anderson 1978: 24).

He uses the term "appropriate weight" – both methods may, indeed must, be used together. This has been largely forgotten over the last two decades.

Polzin, like most other scholars who engage in the literary study of the Bible, builds his house through the destruction of the classical model, just as the Mesopotamian *Enuma Elish* suggests that humanity can only be created from a dead, rebellious god. Granted, it is possible that the similarity of chapters 24 and 26 might frame a mini-unit – I will return to this later – but why must we understand only the mini-unit, ignoring what its building blocks, which show such clear signs of being originally independent units, might have meant before they were "strung together as pearls"? Additionally, why should we view the Bible as a pearl necklace, where each pearl loses its individuality? Perhaps it is more like a charm bracelet, where the individual elements which comprise the whole also retain their identity.

There are other methodological problems with Polzin's approach. He insists that we concentrate on the text as it now stands, on "the discretion and good judgment" of "the story." Why should we not instead, or in addition, ask why the redactor has taken these three stories, which originally meant such and such, and combined them here in this particular fashion, thereby creating a new meaning?

This is a question which is literary–historical in a different sense – it takes seriously the work's textual history, and asks how a redactor, whom more and more critical scholars are recognizing as creative rather than as a hack, might have reworked and reframed earlier materials to convey a message. This strikes me as a significant question, one that the current literary methodologies, which so privilege the synchronic over the diachronic, rarely get to.

The comments made by Polzin and other literary scholars concerning the meaning of these three chapters are accomplished on the basis of a certain amount of violence to the text, because contrary to their claims, chapters 24–6 do not form a neat unit (McCarter 1980: 386–7). The previous chapters had noted how David had fled from Saul; 22:1, for example, notes how David fled to the Adullam cave – why separate that cave adventure from the cave story in chapter 24? More seriously, chapter 26, which narrates the Ziphites "telling on" David to Saul, who was in Gibeah, clearly continues 23: 19, which reads: "Some Ziphites went up to Saul in Gibeah and said, 'David is hiding among us in the strongholds of Horesh, at the hill of Hachilah south of Jeshimon.'" Thus, chapters 24–6 do not from a formal perspective form a single unit.

Polzin, typifying an approach taken by many literary scholars of biblical narrative, privileges the thematic when determining the structure of units. He ignores other more formal criteria. Although more research needs to be done concerning defining the definition of the boundaries of biblical stories (Gottlieb 1991: 214–15),[9] thematic considerations should be secondary to formal criteria. (Due to the highly formalized structure of Judges, the issue of delimiting the boundaries of units will not be as central as it is, for example, in Genesis or Samuel.)

Polzin's study is certainly not the only one to see chapters 24–6 as a unit; this is done in most of the other Samuel-as-literature studies. Yet, each of these authors finds a different theme for this material. Polzin suggests that these chapters teach patience – thus his chapter title "Providential Delays." David had been promised the kingship, and must wait, which tells all Israel in exile to wait patiently; it "keeps a continually disobedient Israel upon the stage long enough for a magnificent history to be written" (Polzin 1989: 214). Miscall is most interested in the personality of David, and deals with these chapters within that framework under the rubric "restraint" (Miscall 1986: 144). Garsiel, whose main focus, as his title suggests, is in what we may learn from juxtaposed texts, highlights the way that the juxtaposition clarifies the various personal qualities of David in opposition to Nabal (Garsiel 1985: 122–3).[10] The comparison of the interpretations of Polzin, Miscall, and Garsiel also highlights the way that each interpreter feels obligated to offer a new interpretation that rarely overlaps with what has earlier been suggested.

Each of these interpretations is rather one-dimensional, high-lighting a single aspect of the text's structure or theme. The biblical literature was written late in ancient near eastern antiquity – in the Iron Age, during the Egyptian New Kingdom, in the Neo-Assyrian and Neo-Babylonian period and beyond, centuries after complex literature like the Epic of Gilgamesh or the New Kingdom love poetry was written. Are we to naïvely believe that the biblical authors were so flat, so monolithic, writing for a single purpose, utilizing a single theme only?

A significant portion of literary studies of biblical texts also have a (tacit) religious motivation – the text is divine in the sense of perfectly structured literature. This has sometimes created what James Barr called over twenty-five years ago an "unholy alliance" between literary scholars and those who oppose historical–critical study on theological grounds (Barr 1973a: 65). Barr notes the certain irony of this development, because, after all, literary study of texts tends to remove them from their referents; but these referents are the source of traditional religiosity (Barr 1973a: 52–74; 1973b: 57).

In sum, most literary studies of biblical material lack depth – precisely the quality that B. Anderson in his 1978 article hoped the new literary studies would bring. They do not ask the most basic questions which may integrate literary and biblical studies, because the literary approach is typically new-critical, structuralist, reader-response, or deconstructionist. In other words, the literary approaches employed allow little room for the history of the text's development and the history that stands behind, or in front of, the text. Thus, the following questions are not typically asked in contemporary literary studies of biblical texts: Who wrote the text? Why? When and where did he live? What were his religious and political views? What other texts and ideas might he have been polemicizing against?

In criticizing certain practices of literary scholars who have explored the Hebrew Bible, I do not intend to ally myself with T.S. Eliot, who calls those who study the Bible solely as literature "parasites" and "pests" (Eliot 1936: 95; Barr 1973b: 12). Nor do I mean to suggest that all other more "traditional" types of literary study of biblical texts are wrong. It all depends on what game (of literary interpretation) you are playing and what rules you opt to use – though I really wish that more practitioners of literary methods were clearer about their rules, so we might actually know if they are playing by the rules, and have won. I am interested in rules which show sensitivity, to the extent possible, to the contexts in which a work was composed as well as its underlying rhetoric. Nor do I mean, by highlighting Fokkelman, Polzin, and Alter, who are predominantly new-critical, to suggest that all literary readings of the Bible belong to that school; certainly other "newer" types of readings have found their way into biblical studies, but these too typically take as a premise that when the Bible is interpreted as literature the history of the text and the place of the author are not significant factors (Exum and Clines 1993; Barr 1973a: 63–4).

In contrast, some of the approaches developed within the New Historicism, or cultural poetics, are useful for engaging biblical historical texts, precisely because this approach takes the context of the literary work seriously. As Robert Carroll noted in reference to the New Historicism and biblical studies: "the Bible is a complex collection of historically embedded texts and textually embedded histories which cries out for a theoretically sophisticated scrutiny" (Carroll 1997: 302). Several of the fundamental principles used by the leading New Historicist critic, Stephen Greenblatt, are easily applied to the Hebrew Bible. Indeed, some of his rules, such as "There can be no motiveless creation" and "There can be no expression without an origin and an object, a *from* and a *for*" (Greenblatt 1988: 12), seem just as essential for biblical interpretation as they might be for understanding Shakespeare.

Ideological criticism also contextualizes the "literary" work in its "historical" milieu (Yee 1995: 146–70). This approach tends to be overly dogmatic, reducing much (or all) of literature to ideology, ignoring other aspects of the text and of literary production. Yet, ideology does play a very extensive role in biblical historical texts (Brettler 1995: 12–14), which as we saw in the previous chapter were not written as detached descriptions of the past. Thus, used with moderation, the insights of these developing branches of biblical and general literary studies will be employed for Judges, because when combined with other approaches, they add appropriate depth to the text.

The questions I am asking and the methods I am advocating are not totally new. Hermann Gunkel, at the turn of the century, also tried to combine the study of the historical and the aesthetic. In the introduction to his Genesis commentary (Gunkel 1994: 27–62), he wrote a section called "The Artistic Forms of the Stories in Genesis"; he was interested, ultimately, in writing a literary history of the Hebrew Bible, and believed that a better understanding of biblical texts would result "if beside critical insight, which until now has so often alone guided the scholar, discerning appreciation should be given a place" (*apud* Hahn 1966: 121). It is noteworthy that in his Genesis commentary, Gunkel was not merely somewhat source-critical, but actually presented the narratives of Genesis as three separate stories – in separate J, E, and P versions! This did not stop him, however, from making literary observations about each of these strands. Furthermore, as a form-critic, he looked at the variant stories in Genesis, and tried to explain, often based on their *Sitze im Leben*, why such similar stories could take such different forms in different contexts.

Modern literary study of the Bible, in its urge to be an Orpah, turning its back on all, has lost sight of these valuable insights and methods of Gunkel. For example, various questions which it seems to me we should ask, and might even begin to answer, are: Why are the "identical" stories in 1 Samuel 24 and 26 shaped differently? Why are they set in different places? Why do they have different amounts of dialogue? Why does one have a humorous bathroom scene in which David cuts off the cloak of Saul's garment while he is exposing himself, while in the second, a magical "deep sleep from the Lord" (1 Sam 26:12) falls upon Saul's camp, so that David may steal Saul's javelin and water dish? (Koch 1969: 132–48; McCarter 1980: 386–7). These questions have some place in a literary reading of this material, but they have been excluded, since (1) a holistic reading does not allow the question to be asked; and (2) the reading I am suggesting uses tools of form-criticism – and these tools are fundamentally *verboten*.

But Gunkel's approach has to a large extent been overlooked by most biblical scholars. Furthermore, the form-critical venture, largely originated by him, has been soundly rejected by most "literary" scholars – the way in which Polzin rather sarcastically dismisses Klaus Koch is typical. This is especially unfortunate. Too often literary scholars have reinvented the wheel, but given it a different name; how distant, for example, are Alter's type-scenes from the *Gattungen* of a German form-critic?

The possible interconnections between various types of ways in which the Bible might be studied have been explored again more recently in the collected essays of the 1994 Kampen workshop, *Synchronic or Diachronic* (de Moor 1995) as well as several studies by James Barr, John Barton and Mark Brett, and the exploration of Paul R. Noble, "Synchronic and Diachronic Approaches to Biblical Interpretation" (Noble 1993). Burke Long in a 1991 survey of literary studies discussed the synchronic versus the diachronic, and noted that "the polarity is misleading" (Long 1991: 77). Several years later, in the inaugural issue of *Biblical Interpretation*, Rolf Rendtorff similarly noted "that we should relate new, mainly synchronic aspects, to older, mainly diachronic insights, for what was observed in careful studies during the last two centuries is not entirely wrong" (Rendtorff 1993: 52). At about the same time, John Barton proclaimed, correctly to my mind, that "historical critics and literary interpreters of the Old Testament already have more in common than they are prepared to acknowledge" (Barton 1994: 10). Indeed, several scholars who have been trained in the historical critical method have produced sensitive, synthetic, hyphenated literary–historical work (Geller 1996; Carr 1996; Talstra 1993).

These scholars, however, are in the minority; few are interested in exploring how various methods that are often felt to be in competition with one another may be employed "to cooperate effectively," to use a phrase of Eep Talstra (Talstra 1998: 13). Mark Minor, who has produced two very useful annotated bibliographies on *Literary–Critical Approaches to the Bible* thus accurately speaks of "a deeper gulf between the two schools [literary and historical–critical] of criticism" (Minor 1992: xix).[11] Mark Brett has similarly noted that biblical scholarship is now typified by "conflicts about method" (Brett 1990: 357).

Let me conclude in typical biblical style, by returning to the beginning – though I must point out that employment of this stylistic device does not make this chapter "Literature." The dichotomy of Huizinga can no longer be accepted; we must recognize that biblical *historical* texts do contain the "element of play" that he felt characterizes literature. These texts also contain at least some structural devices; scholars have even shown this in Chronicles, often considered a boring, unaesthetic work from Israel's "siver age."[12] But, I would suggest, these might very well be schemas rather than tropes; they do not automatically make chapters or books into "Literature." Often, as in most writing, that is, in literature in its etymological sense, structural devices contribute to meaning, and these should be isolated if we want to understand the composition under consideration – but this is equally true of form letters. Thus, the discovery of certain compositional techniques, and what others, especially Barton,[13] have called "literary competence," is crucial for understanding the Bible. This must be done even if we do not characterize the Bible with the honorific "Literature."

There is a certain irony here – the Bible, which is not Literature, has literary devices, and deserves to be read with literary competence.

This irony has created a great deal of confusion and muddiness, especially concerning what the words literature and literary mean when applied to biblical literature. Perhaps we should shun the noun literature and even the adjective literary, so that this confusion is avoided, and we should speak of rhetorical or stylistic devices, which exist in all types of texts, even those which we do not characterize as literary. Alternatively, we must be careful to state that by literature, we only mean something written.

In offering these suggestions, I do not mean to suggest that aesthetic factors never play a role in biblical texts. I think that sociobiology offers a useful analogy (E.O. Wilson 2000); just as certain physical features are retained because of the fundamental interest of the organism in perpetuating itself, the Bible at points was interested in its self-preservation. The aesthetic qualities of a text are *one factor* that might help in this regard. There is a good reason why most of the historical texts do not look like 1 Kings 4 and 6–7. A similar point is made by Peter Ackroyd in reference to Samuel, when he claims that "the sheer joy of telling a story ... *could be a factor* [emphasis added – MZB] in the preservation of many ancient traditions in Israel" (Ackroyd 1971: 6–7).

It is easy to imagine various reasons why the type of literary-historical reading proposed might be rejected out of hand by many biblical scholars. Some might argue, perhaps under the influence of the Copenhagen school (see above, p. 7), that there really is very little agreement about the "real" history of Israel, making this type of contextualized literary study impossible. I disagree. More likely, sustained work will show that the Copenhagen school is using unrealistically stringent standards for reconstructing the history of antiquity. Others might believe that reading is a fundamentally subjective venture. They might even point to the seemingly intractable debate between Meir Sternberg, and David Gunn and Dana Nolan Fewell on how a seemingly straightforward story, Genesis 34, should be read (Sternberg 1985, 1992; Fewell and Gunn 1991). However, all is not in the eye of the beholder, or reader. I am not alone here; Paul Noble in his analysis of this debate concerning the interpretation of Genesis 34 notes: "by careful attention to the linguistic details one can move toward an objective, reader-independent understanding of the text" (Noble 1996: 201). I concur. Methods which have competed in the past must now be used side-by-side, since "the Old Testament contains some very strange literature; perhaps it would not be surprising if it takes more than one kind of sensibility to understand it" (Barton 1994:

15).[14] In the following chapters, I will try to combine in different ways the sensitivities typically associated with historical and with literary study of texts as I explore various episodes in Judges, and also examine the way that we may look at both the separate stories and the complete book. The utility of this eclectic method may be evaluated by others using at least two different criteria: Are the assumptions made about these texts reasonable? Are the readings that result from these assumptions at least as compelling as the alternative interpretations of other scholars?

3

THE SHORT STORY

It is commonly accepted that the core section of the book of Judges, 2:11–16:31, which describes the judges[1] and their activities, is composed of various types of material. It contains two groups of narratives about "minor judges" in 10:1–5 and 12:8–15. These all share a common form of listing the judge, how long he ruled, and where he was buried. Sometimes additional family data is included, but no information is ever given that describes in what sense "he judged Israel" (10:2, 3; 12:9, 11, 14). The origin of these notes and their meaning continues to be debated; it is unclear if these "minor judges" had a role that is different than those of the "major judges," such as Ehud or Samson, or if they might have played a similar function, but were described by a different person in a different way (Mullen 1982: 185–201; Lemche 1983: 47–55). This issue is intractable due to the paucity of evidence, and for this reason, the "minor judges" will not play a significant role in this study.

Unlike the "minor judges," the texts which narrate the stories of the "major judges" are not uniform. This is immediately evident by comparing the length of the stories; the exploits of Othniel are narrated in five verses (3:7–11), while those of Samson occupy four chapters comprised of ninety-one verses (chapters 13–16). The difference between these two is not merely in length; several of the stories, such as the Samson material, are clearly composite. A group of stories about an individual have been edited together, forming a cycle of stories (Amit 1999: 222). This is also clearly the case with the Gideon stories, as evidenced by the alternation between the names Gideon and Jerubbaal, as well as other features which distinguish two groups of stories that have been combined (Amit 1999: 222–66). Judges 4 and 5 are complex in a different way – they include "alternate" tellings in different genres of the "same" story. Thus, in order to understand the core section of Judges, it is important to look at these three genres: the short story, the narrative cycle, and the story comprised of prose and poetic parallels. This will be accomplished in chapters 3–5.

I am understanding the short story in contradistinction to the cycle, thus any story (outside of the minor judges), no matter how long or short, qualifies as a short story as long as it does not show signs of being composite.[2] The narratives of Othniel, Ehud, and Shamgar in chapter 3 are short stories, showing no significant signs of being composite. The story of Shamgar is only one verse long (3:31), but he does not fit into the pattern of the "minor judges," and thus belongs in the category of short stories.[3] The focus of this chapter will thus be on these three short stories, found early in the book.

In examining these three stories, I will focus on the central questions: Why were they composed? What did they mean? How might the structure and historical background of each story contribute to its meaning? In addressing these questions, I will examine whether each story originally existed as a separate narrative before it became incorporated into Judges, in which case I will explore the story's meaning as a separate narrative, without considering its relation to the rest of the book. Given the background of the previous two chapters, these questions about composition and meaning become particularly pressing. We can no longer say that the stories in chapter 3 were written "simply" to reflect what happened, nor is it appropriate to claim that they were composed as literature which should be examined only in terms of structure or technique.

Juxtaposing these three stories will also highlight the diverse nature of stories incorporated into Judges. Even adjacent stories may have very different underpinnings, and may have been written by different people, at different times, for very different reasons. This brings to the fore a central issue of this book, which will be dealt with in detail in the final chapter: Should we read as a whole a book which incorporates such a diversity of material? If so, how?

The Shamgar Narrative

I begin with the shortest, and the most straightforward of these stories, concerning Shamgar (3:31). It is so short, and so lacking in detail, that it is best characterized as a narrative rather than a story (Scholes 1981: 206): "After him came Shamgar son of Anath, who slew six hundred Philistines with an oxgoad. He too was a champion of

Israel." The structure of this episode and of the surrounding material makes it very clear that this verse came into being relatively late in the construction of Judges. Judg 4:1, the introduction to the Deborah-Barak story which now immediately follows the Shamgar narrative, reads: "The Israelites again did what was offensive to YHWH – Ehud now being dead." The story of Ehud is narrated immediately before the verse about Shamgar; the fact that 4:1 notes "Ehud now being dead" rather than "Shamgar now being dead" clearly indicates that at some earlier stage of the composition of Judges, 4:1 immediately followed 3:30 (Lindars 1995: 156).

Its length is not the only feature that makes 3:31 exceptional. All of the narratives of the major judges begin with a note about Israel doing what is evil in YHWH's eyes, and most conclude with a note about the land being "tranquil" for a period of time. These distinguishing features are absent in the Shamgar account, which instead is loosely attached to what precedes by beginning "After him" and noting later in the verse "He too." All of this evidence suggests that 3:31 was added after the main structure of Judges, comprised of the series of major judges surrounded by notes of sin, punishment, calling out to God, God raising a judge who saved Israel, and the land remaining tranquil for a period of time, was already in place.[4]

The conclusions just noted are broadly accepted, as is the observation that the Shamgar narrative is based on Judges 5:6a: "In the days of Shamgar son of Anath, in the days of Jael, caravans ceased." An editor of Judges most likely puzzled over this reference to Shamgar in the Song of Deborah, and resolved his quandary by assuming that Shamgar would only be worthy of mention if he was an important figure, likely a judge. This puzzlement was solved by writing Shamgar into the text in 3:31, immediately before the period of Deborah, so he could be alive as a contemporary of Jael when the reader reached the Deborah–Barak material in chapters 4–5.

But where did the additional information about Shamgar come from? Specifically, how did this anonymous author–editor[5] "know" that he "slew six hundred Philistines with an oxgoad"?

Most likely, the idea that Shamgar saved Israel specifically from the Philistines derives from Judg 10:11, where YHWH tells Israel that he had rescued them "from the Egyptians, from the Amorites, from the Ammonites, and from the Philistines."[6] However (with the exception of 3:31), no earlier text of Judges tells of Israel being saved from the Philistines. Especially given that the name Shamgar is non-Semitic (*HALOT* 4:1552, s.v. שמגר), and likely would have been recognized as such even in antiquity, it is obvious how an ancient historian would have put together the evidence from Judg 5:6 and 10:11 to conclude that Shamgar was a judge who rescued the Israelites from the Philistines at the time of Jael.

It is less clear where the historian derived the "knowledge" that this victory was accomplished using an oxgoad and involved the slaying of six hundred people. Six hundred is a good traditional ballpark figure for the number of Philistines an individual might kill single-handedly, as seen from the numbers of three to eight hundred killed by David's warriors in 2 Samuel 23 (vv. 8, 18). Perhaps the author was also aware of traditions concerning unusual "ammunition" used in Israelite–Philistine battles, ranging from Samson's donkey jaw (Judg 15:15–17), to Goliath's spear, which "had a shaft like a weaver's bar" (1 Sam 17:7; 2 Sam 21:19) – this may stand behind the oxgoad tradition. Alternatively, the Hebrew of the implement mentioned in 3:31 might also be translated as "*the* oxgoad,"[7] raising the possibility that it is an etiological reference based on a story that developed around a particular oxgoad that might have appeared bloodied, or might have looked like a particularly good weapon; this would explain how an oxgoad became attracted to the story of Shamgar the Philistine slayer.

Though the origin of part of the tradition in 3:31 is guesswork, it is significant that at least some of the Shamgar material clearly originates as interpretation of earlier texts. It never was a self-standing tradition, and developed in this form only after an earlier form of the Book of Judges existed. The authors of biblical historical texts were historians in the sense of being aware of, and interpreting, earlier traditions. This does not mean that the Shamgar note is true; the historian might very well have misinterpreted his source, and likely has embellished it imaginatively. What is important is that the single verse shows that one of the factors responsible for material that eventually became part of the book of Judges was the interpretation of texts already in the book.

The Othniel Story

The genesis of the Othniel story in 3:7–11 was discussed briefly in chapter 1 (see above, pp. 4–5). It "is universally recognized to be a Dtr composition without a basis in an earlier book of Judges" (Lindars 1995: 99). Even though in length and structure it is different from the Shamgar material, like that verse, it never existed before the composition of some form of the book of Judges. The

fact that it was written for the book is especially clear from its highly formulaic nature, which exactly matches the paradigm offered in
2:11–19, as well as the introduction and conclusion of many of the
major judge units. The formulaic nature of the passage is made
clear below by using roman type for phrases attested elsewhere in
Judges (Amit 1999: 161–3) and printing in italic phrases not found
in Judges, but characteristic of Dtr literature. This clearly illustrates
that this story is one of the most stereotypic passages in the entire
Hebrew Bible:

> (7) The Israelites did what was offensive to YHWH; *they
> forgot YHWH their God*[8] and worshiped the Baalim *and
> the Asheroth*. (8) YHWH became incensed at Israel and
> surrendered them to Cushan-rishathaim king of Aram-
> naharaim; and the Israelites were subject to Cushan-
> rishathaim for eight years. (9) The Israelites cried out to
> YHWH, and YHWH raised a champion for the Israelites
> and he delivered them: Othniel the Kenizzite, a younger
> kinsman of Caleb. (10) The spirit of YHWH descended
> upon him and he judged Israel. *He went out to war, and
> YHWH delivered* King Cushan-rishathaim of Aram *into his
> hand;* he prevailed over[9] Cushan-rishathaim, (11) and the
> land had peace for forty years; then Othniel the Kenizzite
> died.

As should be clear, only the name of the protagonist, "Othniel the
Kenizzite, a younger kinsman of Caleb," and the name and country of the defeated king, "Cushan-rishathaim (of) Aram-naharaim"
are not part of the stereotypic language that the author would have
known. The name Othniel, in fact, the whole phrase "Othniel the
Kenizzite, a younger kinsman of Caleb," is taken verbatim from
Josh 15:17 (//Ju 1:13).[10] Othniel is chosen as a judge by our author
for several reasons: (1) According to the account in Joshua 15, he
captures and smites, two activities which typify judges in Judges;
(2) Since he comes from the period of Joshua, he is an ideal figure
as a first judge, effecting the transition between the conquest and
the period of judges (Lindars 1995: 128); (3) He is related to Caleb,
and was thus understood to be a Judean (Fretz and Panitz 1992:
809; Kuntz 1992: 17). There is no other Judean judge in the book;
given the likely time of composition or certainly the time of final
editing of Judges, after the destruction of the northern kingdom
(18:30), this needed to be rectified. Moreover, a heroic Judean

Othniel fits the author's paradigm of ideal Judean leadership (see below, pp. 88–9, 97–102, 110–16).

The choice of the name of both person and place – "Cushan-rishathaim (of) Aram-naharaim" – is strange on several grounds. The personal name Cushan-rishathaim, "dark, double-wicked" does not fit the patterns of Semitic name-giving, which typically exalt some aspect of a deity, often in relation to the birth of a child (Fowler 1988). Any Israelite reader was likely to pick up on the strangeness of the name, which I believe was meant to offer a type of textual clue for how to read the story.

The designation of the area of Syria as Aram-naharaim is equally strange. Syria is typically called Aram; Aram-naharaim appears only four other times in the Bible (Gen 24:10; Deut 23:5; Ps 60:2; 1Chr 19:6). Indeed, in 3:10, and later in the book, in 10:6, the area is called Aram, rather than Aram–Naharaim. In addition, as observed earlier, it is very strange that Judah, a southern tribe, should fight the Arameans, to the north. Finally, it is unusual that Aram-naharaim and Cushan-rishathaim rhyme. This would be particularly noteworthy in ancient Israel, where end-rhyme did not exist as a convention, though it could be used for its heightening effects.[11]

When considered together, these various factors – the highly stereotypical nature of the narration, the name of the enemy and the designation of his country, the adoption of a well-known Judean hero, the geographical improbabilities, and the end-rhyme – suggest that this story was not meant as history in the sense of a narration of *the* past. It lacks verisimilitude on too many levels to function as that type of history. Instead, it was meant as a type of allegory for the ability of a good, righteous Judean judge to defeat the wicked enemy "from the North."

The story is allegorical in the most general sense of "say[ing] one thing and mean[ing] another" (Fletcher 1964: 2). "Contextual consideration within the linguistic semantics, the literary context, the cultural background and the historical setting" (Barr 1989b: 16) suggest that particular biblical stories should be read allegorically. In this case, its stereotypical structure, odd names and geographical improbabilities suggest that it is doing something other than representing a real war between Othniel and Cushan-rishathaim.

This story is not unique as an allegory that is set in the past, and thus *looks* historical. The book of Ruth, with its symbolically named characters, which begins by narrating a famine in the house of bread (Bethlehem) is also marked as being allegorical rather than historical in the sense of accurately depicting *the* past. Yet, like our passage in Judges, it conveys a set of very important teachings, both about the significance of acts of loving-kindness (חסד) and about the ability of a foreigner to integrate into the community. Allegory is a significant method used by biblical historians in their construction of history.

Like 3:31, this episode of Othniel the judge was created from earlier traditions – it used the framework paradigm (2:11–19), the frameworks of the individual judges' stories, and the tradition concerning Othniel in Joshua to create a model Judean judge. But in other ways, it is fundamentally unlike Judg 3:31. On the simplest level it is longer, but ironically, it is much more stereotypical and less creative. More significantly, it really is of a different genre; if I have read the textual clues properly, then 3:31 is meant to tell of a real judge named Shamgar who defeated real Philistines, while 3:7–11 are meant to reflect on Judean superiority, using the literary fiction of "Cushan-rishathaim of Aram-naharaim." It is striking that two such dissimilar stories, clearly written by two different authors, are in such close proximity to each other.

The Ehud Story[12]

The story of Ehud's defeat of Eglon king of Moab in Judg 3:12–30 separates the two stories just analyzed: [13]

> (12) The Israelites again did what was evil[14] in the eyes of YHWH; YHWH empowered Eglon, King of Moab, against Israel because they did what was evil in the eyes of YHWH. (13) He mobilized the Ammonites and the Amalekites under him; when he went and attacked Israel, they conquered the City of Datepalms. (14) The Israelites were vassals of Eglon King of Moab for eighteen years. (15) The Israelites cried out to YHWH, and YHWH established a savior for them, Ehud son of Gera, a Benjaminite, a left-handed man; the Israelites sent tribute in his hand to Eglon King of Moab. (16) Ehud made himself a sword – it was double-edged and short; he girded it under his garments on his right hip. (17) He "sacrificed" the tribute-offering to Eglon, King of Moab. Incidentally, Eglon was a very corpulent man. (18) As he finished "sacrificing" his tribute-offering, he dismissed (his) retainers, the tribute bearers. (19) He had just returned from Pesilim, which is

near Gilgal. He said, "I have a secret matter concerning you, O king." He said, "Quiet!" All of his retainers left him. (20) Ehud had come to him while he was sitting in the throne room which was his private room. When Ehud said, "I have a divine oracle concerning you," he arose from the throne. (21) Ehud moved his left hand, took the sword from his right thigh, and stuck it into his belly. (22) The hilt followed the blade, and fat surrounded the blade because he did not remove the sword from his belly; and the excrement came out. (23) Ehud left toward the portico(?); he closed the doors of the throne room behind himself, and locked them. (24) Just as he had left, [Eglon's] servants came, and they noticed – the doors of the throne room were locked. They said, "He must be "covering his legs"[15] in the throne room. (25) They waited until the point of embarrassment, but he still did not open the doors of the throne room. They took the key, and opened it, and there was their master sprawled on the ground, dead. (26) Meanwhile, Ehud had fled while they were waiting. He had passed Pesilim, on his way to Seir. (27) When he arrived, he blew a shofar on Mount Ephraim. The Israelites descended the mountain with him, with him in the lead. (28) He said to them, "Follow me, for YHWH has given your enemies, the Moabites into your hands"; they followed him, and captured the Jordan crossings that belonged to Moab, and let no one pass. (29) They smote the Moabites at that time, about ten thousand men, every fat man and every warrior; not one fled. (30) Moab was subjugated on that day under the hand of the Israelites; the land was then at peace for eighty years.

This story has been the subject of some significant studies of the Bible as literature. Sternberg uses it to illustrate "the art of the proleptic epithet" (Sternberg 1985: 328–37). Alonso-Schökel in his study of "*Erzählkunst*" (narrative art) from 1961, one of the pioneering works of the literary study of the Bible, noted devices such as the repetition of words and phrases, including the story's use of "hand" as a *Leitwort*, and the rhythmic nature of much of the story (Alonso-Schökel 1961: 149–57). Alter's analysis of the Ehud story in his influential *The Art of Biblical Narrative* emphasizes its mimetic nature, its use of punning, name symbolism (especially Eglon, "a play on *ʿégel*, calf [who] turns out to be a fatted calf ready for slaughter"), prefiguration (תקע in vv. 21, 27, used of thrusting the dagger and blowing the shofar to rally the troops) and scatological and sexual references (the bathroom incident, dagger thrusts, locked doors) (Alter 1981: 38–41; Jull 1988: 63–75). He alludes to a similarity between the Ehud story and "satire in the time of war," and notes:

> In all this, as I have said, it is quite possible that the writer faithfully represents the historical data without addition or substantive embellishment. The organization of the narrative, however … produce[s] an imaginative reenactment of the historical event, conferring upon it a strong attitudinal definition and discovering in it a pattern of meaning. It is perhaps less historicized fiction than fictionalized history – history in which the feeling and the meaning of events are concretely realized through the technical resources of prose fiction.
>
> (Alter 1981: 40)

The analyses of Sternberg, Alonso-Schökel and Alter are different attempts at understanding the Ehud story as literature. Some biblical scholars have developed their observations, concluding as well that the main goal of the story was "to entertain the hearers" (Lindars 1995: 139). In contrast, I would like to explore a historical–critical reading which contextualizes the work in ancient Israel.

It is difficult to know which of the devices noted by each scholar were actually perceived in ancient Israel, that is, to use a term popularized by John Barton, which were part of the Israelite "literary competence" (see above, p. 19). Literary devices depend on conventions which vary widely between cultures and within individual cultures at different times. We can list particular devices and phonological features, but their perception is culturally and historically determined. In addition, even when we believe a particular structure existed and was perceived by ancient readers or listeners of the story, we should not immediately call texts showing such patterns "literary," a word which typically implies a positive aesthetic judgement. Rather, as noted in Chapter Two, we should inquire after the purpose of the unusual patterning or word choice.

One pattern that runs throughout the unit is the use of sacrificial terminology. This was noted by Alonso-Schökel, Alter and Amit, who comment on the sacrificial overtones in Eglon's name, from ʿégel, "a calf." (Amit 1999: 183–4; G.P. Miller 1996: 114–15). This observation, however, requires additional strengthening, since animal names are used of other biblical characters – indeed the Judean spy Caleb has such a name ("dog"), which seems to play no symbolic role in that narrative.

In the case of the Ehud narrative, further careful stylistic analysis provides additional sacrificial terminology. Vv. 17 and 18, in saying that Ehud offered tribute, use an expression typically used of offering a sacrifice (Amit 1999: 184 n. 19). This exceptional and inappropriate use of animal sacrifice terminology would likely have led the ancient Israelite reader or listener to conclude that sacrifice is an underlying theme of the passage. This is why I translated v. 17 as, "He 'sacrificed' the tribute-offering." The author's choice of this idiom suggests that the name Eglon is symbolic, and highlights its sacrificial overtones. The story as a whole plays on the notion of sacrifice: while pretending "to bring tribute"/"offering" to Eglon, it is actually Eglon, "the calf," who becomes the offering. Indeed, the sacrificial knife and the partial disembowelment of the "animal" are depicted in graphic detail. The likelihood of this sacrificial interpretation is enhanced by seeing how it fits the rest of the story.

Alter noted certain aspects of the narrative's scatology and "deliberate sexual nuance" (Alter 1981: 39). The text explicitly refers to Eglon's excrement (v. 22) and his servants' assumption that he is relieving himself (v. 24). In addition, as Alter notes, the thrust of the dagger may be viewed sexually. These observations may be further extended through a closer reading of the story and an analysis of the terms that its author chose to use.

We know relatively little about ancient Israelite sexual terminology, particularly sexual slang. The Ehud story, however contains several phrases which are elsewhere found in explicitly sexual contexts. For example, disproportionate space is given to the opening and closing of doors (vv. 23–5). This certainly develops the story, but also introduces a set of words that are well-anchored in metaphors for sexuality in ancient Israel. These include the use of "to open" and "locked," which are used sexually in Cant 5:5 and 4:12. The possible sexual significance of Ehud's sword in v. 16, as short and double-edged, namely as a short straight sword, gains credence once we realize that the typical sword of the period had a curved side with which one hacks away at enemies, and thus was much less appropriate as a phallic symbol. Furthermore, in v. 20, the author uses the expression "come to" to express Ehud's approach toward Eglon; this term may also be used of sexual intercourse. Finally, the "formulaic" ending in v. 30 is slightly different from the similar formulae in Judges in that it contains the word "hand." Certainly, in this context its primary meaning is "hand," but elsewhere, it is used euphemistically for the penis. It is possible that the choice to break with the typical pattern and to insert "hand" was informed by an awareness that what stands behind it is the sexual subjugation of the Moabites to the Israelites. If this is so, an editor of Judges who rounded out the story by adding this formulaic comment appreciated the sexual aspect of Eglon's subjugation, and slightly modified the usual conclusion to fit that image.

This sexual reading should not be viewed as a product of modern, post-Freudian sensibilities. An explicitly sexual medieval poem of Todros Abulafiah ends, "Oh how I wish – may she come to me and the hilt will penetrate after the blade."[16] The reuse of Judg 3:22 in this poem shows that the sexual imagery that stands behind this chapter was already appreciated in the thirteenth century.

Judg 3:12–30, almost from the beginning, sets up the Moabite enemy as a sacrificial victim. It is full of scatological and sexual references at the enemy's expense. Recognition of these features certainly makes the chapter more pleasurable for us to read, and might have been perceived as pleasurable in antiquity as well. But I would argue that looking at these devices in terms of their likely aesthetic use is overly narrow. The typical readings ignore the fact that a specifically Moabite king is chosen here. This suggests that the story should be read more broadly in the context of Israelite–Moabite relations.

Ideally, we should present the relationship between the two nations during the period of the story's composition. This is impossible, however, because it does not contain sufficient clues about when it was written, although the story's setting in the period of the judges is certainly anachronistic. Most scholars would agree that the Book of Judges was redacted at the latest in the early exilic period, incorporating earlier traditions, some of which originated as tribal stories (O'Connell 1996: 345–68). Thus, in order to understand the story's stylistic features in relation to its author's historical background, it is relevant to sketch the evidence concerning the relations between Moab and Israel in the pre-exilic period.

The vast majority of evidence suggests hostility between the neighbors. This is reflected in many types of stories. Torah texts such as the oracles of Balaam in Num 21:29 and 24:17, and the legislation of Deut 23:4 reflect this enmity. According to "historical texts," the Moabites were vassals already at the time of David (2 Sam 8:2), and battles between Moab and Israel are narrated in 2 Kgs 1:1; 3:4–27; 13:20 and 24:2. The Moabites are condemned in collections of oracles against the nations from the beginning through the end of classical prophecy (Amos 2:1–3; Isaiah 15–16; Jeremiah 48 and Ezek 25:8–11). Antipathy is also reflected in Ps 60:10 (=108:10) and 83:7. Taken as a group, these texts point to the existence of antagonism between Moab and Judah and Israel for much of the pre-exilic period. This perspective is also confirmed by the Moabite Mesha Stele, which mentions Israelite oppression of Moab for "many days" (line 5), and follows this with a depiction of Moabite conquest of Israelite territory (Pritchard 1955: 320).

Given the sexual overtones of the Ehud–Eglon story, the story of Moab's birth from an incestuous father–daughter relationship (Gen 19:37) is of particular interest. Numbers 25 also describes Moabite women enticing Israelite men; v. 8 describes impaling one of the offending Moabite women through the genitals (Milgrom 1990: 215). Thus, a particular interest in Moabite sexuality is part of the broader likely background of the story in Judges.[17]

Positive relations between Moab and Israel might be suggested by Deut 2:9, which notes that Israel should not harass Moab when entering the land of Israel, and by 1 Sam 22:3–4, where David leaves his parents with the king of Moab for safekeeping. These two texts, however, are in the minority. They might reflect a relatively brief period of peaceful coexistence between Israel and Moab.

This historical sketch suggests that the story in Judg 3:12–30 should be understood as a humorous satire mocking the Israelites' enemy, the Moabites. Although scholars have claimed that "the holy book we call the Bible revels in profound laughter" (Exum and Whedbee 1984: 6),[18] it is difficult to determine what ancient Israelites actually found funny, since the biblical text rarely contains notices that people laughed after hearing particular types of utterances. Certainly conceptions of what makes contemporary stories funny may not be automatically projected backward on to biblical Israel. It is therefore desirable to understand Israelite humor by using models that do not depend on contemporary Western humor. The discussion of Franz Rosenthal about early Islamic humor is especially useful in this regard (Rosenthal 1956; Foster 1974). Many of the stories which according to Moslem tradition are humorous, are not humorous to us, and this forces Rosenthal to form generalizations about humor that cover both modern and ancient societies. He notes:

> The definition [of humor] which would appear to be the most plausible one because of its general applicability connects humor with the relief felt at the momentary lifting of one of the many restrictions which the physical and social environment imposes upon man.... . The humor in puns ... has its origin in the fact that human linguistic expression moves in quite narrow and circumscribed and usually logical channels. Any deviation from those channels is keenly felt as a release from conventional restrictions and, therefore, is humorous. A great variety of dealings among human beings is immediately classified as humor if there is any suggestion of a deviation from ordinary reality and the conventions of human society.
>
> (Rosenthal 1956: 1)

Some biblical evidence suggests that Rosenthal's conventions are applicable to ancient Israel as well. For example, one of the rare cases when the narrator tells us that someone laughs concerns the laughter of Abraham or Sarah at the impending birth of a son (Gen 17:17; 18:12, 15). They laugh because their old age makes the event highly unlikely – it is a "deviation from ordinary reality."

Seen within Rosenthal's parameters, it is clear that the Ehud story is humorous. Its explicit, extensive use of scatology and its sexual innuendo are a "momentary lifting of one of the many restrictions which the ... social environment imposes upon man." The episode described, with a single commoner defeating the enemy king and outsmarting the royal courtiers, is certainly "a deviation from ordinary reality." Furthermore, if this story was written during one of the periods when Israel was a vassal of Moab, by portraying Israel as the victor it presents a substantial release from everyday life. Thus, what we do know of Israelite culture suggests that this story was appreciated as humorous in antiquity. It was seen as poking fun at Eglon and the Moabites in general, who as noted above, were typically viewed as an out-group from the Israelites' perspective. This type of humor which disparages an out-group typically functions, "(1) To increase the morale and solidify the ingroup [and] (2) To introduce or foster a hostile disposition toward that out-group" (Martineau 1972: 118–19).

Alter and others have suggested that this humorous story be characterized as satire (Alter 1981: 39; Webb 1987: 129–30).[19] This designation raises an issue similar to that of noting that the story is humorous: When is it appropriate to apply to the Bible such genre labels as "satire," which originate in the classical world?

The application of non-native genre labels to ancient texts has been discussed in detail by Tremper Longman III in connection to his isolation of the genre "fictional Akkadian autobiography," (Longman 1991: 3–21; 1987), a label which certainly does not occur in any of the texts that Longman examines. He notes that genre labels perform an invaluable function by guiding the reader in interpreting a work, since interpretation is largely genre-determined, and texts from the same genre are mutually illuminating (Longman 1991: 7, 15–19). Many leading literary scholars, such as Northrop Frye and Tsvetan Todorov would concur (N. Frye 1957: 247–8; Todorov 1976: 163; Madsen 1994: 7–27). Ralph Cohen, in a defense of the concept "genre," notes that this function is true for literature of any period, oral as well as written (Cohen 1986: 206). For example, a person who reads a work written to be a parody as a historical account would be misunderstanding that work's ancient function, and would misinterpret it. (This has been called "generic misfiring" [Cohen 1989: 15].) Given the importance of genre as a guide for reading, Longman claims that it is appropriate to impose genre labels not known to be native to a culture (Longman 1991: 14). Following Gunkel, various criteria, such as mood, vocabulary and social setting might help determine a work's genre (Longman 1991: 13).

The contrary position, that non-native genres should be avoided, is argued by James Kugel in *The Idea of Biblical Poetry: Parallelism and Its History* (Kugel 1981a). He notes that there is no biblical Hebrew word for poetry, and states, "Thus, to speak of 'poetry' at all in the Bible will be in some measure to impose a concept foreign to the biblical world" (Kugel 1981a: 69; cf. 85, 94). However, as noted by Kugel's critics, even though "poetry" is a Greek term, it is appropriate in reference to biblical texts because calling a text "poetry" offers us clues on how to read it (Geller 1982: 75–7; Landy 1984: 68–70). If we read (the "poetic") Isaiah 1 in the same way that we read (the "prosaic") Exodus 1, we would seriously misunderstand Isaiah. We would be stumped by certain syntactic features (such as the frequent omission of the verb in the B line), we might interpret some figurative language literally, and we would not know how to process verses which are constructed using parallelism. By offering the label "poetry" to Isaiah, we help to classify it as not prose, and as similar *in certain significant respects* to varieties of poetry known from our Western civilization.

As modern readers of the biblical texts, we need some term to designate this group of texts and to indicate that it should not be read in the same way as different types of other ("prose") texts, and hence we choose the most helpful of our own terms, "poetry."

Kugel's desire to avoid designating biblical texts as "poetry" is partially motivated by a legitimate concern that we might be anachronistic, and incorrectly impose all of the typical characteristics of non-biblical poetry (e.g. meter) onto the Bible. However, genres are relatively open-ended and flexible, so all works of the same genre need not share all the same characteristics. Defining ancient genres aids us in seeing certain characteristics of a work that were not previously highlighted, and sometimes allows us to presume a likely social setting or role for literary texts.

The psalms of the Bible have been divided on the basis of form-critical features into such genres as laments of the individual, laments of the community, hymns, etc. Hermann Gunkel played a central role in this division, and his categories or genres, which do not reflect biblical terminology, have remained influential. These categories have been recently called into question in H.-J. Kraus' Psalms commentary, where designations actually found in the psalms themselves are preferred.[20] His suggestion has not been generally accepted because Gunkel's model (in a modified form) offers a more useful interpretive tool than Kraus' terms, since its categories help to group together certain psalms with certain terms and characteristics (e.g. the phrase "YHWH is/has become king" or the "confidence motif"), allowing them to be viewed together and to bear on one another.

The genre of satire transcends cultural and chronological boundaries, as noted by Paul Frye: "The satiric spirit as it is manifested in verse seems to appear (whether as mockery, raillery, ridicule, or formalized invective) in the literature or folklore of all peoples, early and late, pre-literate and civilized" (P. Frye 1986: 248). It is found in non-Western literature, where one of its main functions is to offer relief and a feeling of superiority through the use of humor (Feinberg 1972: 33–61). Other biblical scholars have recently collected a significant number of satirical texts in the Bible; the Ehud–Eglon story should be added to their lists (Jemielty 1992; Weisman 1998).

The Ehud story conforms perfectly to the characteristics of satire noted by Northrop Frye: "wit or humor founded on fantasy or a sense of the grotesque or absurd [and] … an object of attack" (N. Frye 1957: 224). The chapter's prominent use of sexual and scatological themes fits its nature as satire, as does its use of animal imagery. The understanding of the Ehud pericope as political satire is particularly relevant to its interpretation because "all satire is not only an attack; it is an attack upon discernible, historically authentic particulars" (Rosenheim 1971: 317–18). This statement emphasizes that the *literary* category of satire has a particular *social–historical* setting, and that the satire in Judg 3:12–30 must be understood within the background provided earlier in this chapter of the actual relationship between Israel and Moab. The story reinforces the out-group identity of Moab, who was geographically proximate to Israel, and according to tradition, related to it (Gen 19:29–38). Such satirical stories were necessary because of the existence of other traditions that suggested a more conciliatory attitude toward the Moabites.

This analysis has an important corollary. Any interpreter who misses the satirical nature of the story is bound to misinterpret and to misuse it. This has specially important implications for the modern biblical historian, since composers of satire typically engage in "distortions, analogies, or 'pure' fabrications" (Rosenheim 1971: 312). Thus, much of the story might be an "invented tradition" (Hobsbawm and Ranger 1983)[21] set in the past. It was composed for political purposes, namely to mock the enemy Moabites, and is not a straightforward representation of historical events. As the ancient reader picked up on the clues suggesting that it is satire, he or she would have realized that this was not historical in the sense that it was trying to recount the real past. Thus, any attempt by modern authors of histories of Israel to use this story for reconstructing the "period of judges" is fundamentally misguided; the genre of this story makes this venture impossible.[22]

Judg 3:12–30 is history only in the sense that it is a narrative that presents a past. The specifics of this past likely have little to do with real Moab; instead, an author has fashioned a creative work of political satire, predominantly reflecting not the history of the period it purports to describe, but the period and conflicts of its author. Certain "literary" motifs, such as the enemy as a sacrificial victim, and scatological and sexual references, had a social function of mocking the real (not the literary) Moabites, who were perceived by the writer as Israel's enemies.

Although this pericope does not narrate factual history, the literary representations it conveys did play a historical role within ancient Israel. To use the insights of the New Historicism, the unit both expresses and furthers the Israelite belief in their superiority over their neighbors, the Moabites.[23] It is a story of national pride, which serves to illustrate the special way in which Israel perceived itself as God's chosen nation, small, but greater than others, and most certainly superior to the petty city-states that surrounded it. It illustrates YHWH's unconditional love for a chosen people that is "the smallest of all the nations" (Deut 7:7).

Not all of the rhetorical elements isolated within the Ehud pericope by various scholars, such as Alonso-Schökel, Alter and Sternberg may be accounted for by understanding the story as satire. Biblical texts, like many writings, are not typically composed for a single purpose. As noted by David Gunn, "Literature that reads like a theological tract or political pamphlet typically has a short life as entertainment" (Gunn 1980: 12). This fits with the notion mentioned earlier that a sociobiological model helps to explain some part of the literary nature of the biblical text (see above, p. 20) – having a useful social or religious function is not always sufficient; if this is combined with being aesthetically satisfying, the chances of being preserved are greater.

We can follow other scholars and point out certain devices that make the Ehud story interesting, fun or aesthetic *to us*. These might include: the use of irony, especially concerning the left-handed Righthander [Benjaminite], the linking of various sections with the root נ/ב used of "thrusting" the dagger (in v. 21), and of "blowing" the shofar (in v. 27), the rhyme between the proximate obscure words *happaršedona*, "the excrement" (v. 22b) and *hammisderona*, "the portico" (v. 23a), and the use of various types of dramatic foreshadowing (Sternberg 1985: 328–37). Much of this section, however, has emphasized the methodological difficulties of knowing whether the modern reading of a biblical work is anachronistic because of difficulties in determining ancient literary competence. For this reason, I am unsure how we might determine whether these devices were used by the ancient author to give his audience pleasure. It is very difficult to "read like an ancient Judahite" (Edelman 1991: 13 and *passim*) in the sense of judging the aesthetic pleasure that the text might have offered to its ancient audience.

The Variety of Short Stories

Though the three narratives of Othniel, Ehud, and Shamgar are adjacent, they are fundamentally different in nature. The Ehud story existed before the Book of Judges came together, and was touched up slightly at its beginning and end to be integrated into the book. In contrast, internal evidence suggests that the Othniel and Shamgar stories were written specifically for the book. Yet, they are very different stories, in terms of length, detail, and creativity. Both the Shamgar and Othniel episodes lack any dialogue or drama, in marked contrast to the Ehud story. Yet the Othniel narrative is a story – it has a beginning, middle, and end, unlike the very laconic note about Shamgar.

The purposes of these three stories are also different. The Othniel story was written as a paradigm illustrating the ideal judge, who comes from Judah. The Ehud story was written as a political satire, to mock the Moabites. The Shamgar story was written as an introduction to the Deborah–Barak story, and is based on textual interpretation. I believe that the three stories are also different in terms of their implied historicity. The Ehud and Othniel stories contain clues that they are not meant to be read as depictions of the real past. In contrast, in the brief Shamgar narrative, the author believes that he is describing the real Shamgar who is mentioned in chapter 5. Thus, even though in their final form these three stories are part of the same book, they should also be read separately, with proper consideration of their unique natures and purposes.

4

THE SAMSON CYCLE

As noted in the previous chapter, several of the stories in Judges are not unified compositions, but are collections of a variety of materials by different authors concerning a single individual. The existence of such cycles incorporating diverse material has long been suspected. In the nineteenth century, many scholars believed that the sources of the Pentateuch or Hexateuch continued in Judges, and used traditional source criticism as the main method for explaining duplication in Judges, with most of the book viewed as a combination of the (early) J and E sources (Moore 1895: xix–xxxvii). With the rise of Martin Noth's model of a Deuteronomistic History extending from Deuteronomy to 2 Kings, this older, source-critical model fell out of use, and was replaced by a model in which a Deuteronomistic editor put various pre-existing stories into a framework, creating (some form of) the Book of Judges. Noth recognized that not all of the stories about each judge are uniform. For example, he suggests that "the long Gideon story (Judg 6:1–8:32) had already been compiled in the old tradition out of various different elements" (Noth 1981:45). Once Judges was sundered from the Hexateuch, isolating such elements became particularly complicated, since the various trademarks of J and E could no longer be used to differentiate between material, although the broad criteria of doublets and contradictions could still be used.

This chapter will concentrate on the Samson material, taking it apart and putting it back together. It will isolate the various building blocks that now comprise the cycle, asking literary–historical questions of each component, particularly seeking out what each section meant by imagining the most likely background that explains each part's structure and content. It will then consider the cycle as a whole, endeavoring to explain how it was composed, and the problem of interpreting it as a whole.

Just as the previous chapter indicated that there was no single model for the short story, each of the cycles has its own composition history. It thus would have been valuable to look at additional cycles, beyond the Samson story. However, this would have turned this work into a commentary, rather than an introductory guide to Judges.

The Composite Nature of the Cycles

Until recently, only internal evidence could be used to determine that several of the units concerning major judges were composite. Such evidence is somewhat subjective; we have no clear information that would determine how much contradiction a single author could tolerate,[1] or when a doublet might be authorial, for emphasis or some other rhetorical purpose, as opposed to indicating multiplicity of authorship. In fact, the scholars highlighted in Chapter Two, who examined the Bible from a literary perspective, went a long way in making various redactors, and thereby sources, disappear (Barton 1996: 56–8), as they found alternative reasons to explain seeming contradictions and duplications.

It is difficult to disprove many of the points raised by literary scholars of the Bible, to show how their readings do not really prove the unity of the works under consideration. Certainly, no one expects to find the separate, original materials from which these cycles have been composed. The subjective nature of any suggestions concerning the materials woven together to form the cycles is immediately evident from the diversity of conflicting suggestions concerning their history of composition – a point often noted by literary scholars, who suggest that this lack of consensus proves that it is better to read the text as a unified whole. Yet, clear evidence now shows that critical scholarship was correct in assuming that some of these stories are cycles, with complex and long histories.

Already in his *Prolegomena*, Wellhausen suggested that Judg 6:7–10 is a secondary "insertion in the last redaction" because in these four verses an anonymous prophet "makes his appearance as suddenly as his withdrawal is abrupt" (Wellhausen 1973: 234). This brilliant conjecture has now been confirmed with the discovery of the Dead Sea Scroll manuscript 4QJudg[a], dating from approximately 50–25 BCE, in which verses 7–10 are missing (Barrera 1989: 229–45; DJD 14:161–4). It is not crucial for our purposes to explain how, when, and why these verses were added; it is simply important to use the Qumran manuscript as incontrovertible evidence that the Book of Judges went through a number of recensions, and that in its current form, it incorporates significant editorial activity.

Unfortunately, only a fragment of 4QJudg[a] has survived, so we cannot know in what other places this manuscript reflected an earlier, shorter text.[2] Yet, in the Samson material, there is very clear internal evidence that a variety of stories have been combined to form a cycle. Judg 13:1, "The Israelites again did what was evil[3] in the eyes of YHWH; YHWH gave them into the hand of the Philistines for forty years," is the Dtr introduction to the story as a whole; it is similar to the introductions of the other major judges (O'Connell 1996: 28–37). In contrast to the Ehud story, where the introduction has replaced the story's original introduction, which is now lost, here 13:1 has been prefixed to the original story, and the original introduction, "There once was a man…," is retained.[4]

The clearest break in the Samson story is at 15:20: "He judged Israel during the time of the Philistines for twenty years." This is an ending formula, and indeed it is repeated in a variant form in 16:31b, "he had judged Israel for twenty years."[5] Such repetitions are characteristic of resumptive repetitions, which have various functions, including marking the intervening material as an insertion (Brettler 1995: 116, 210 nn. 21–2). Thus, internal evidence suggests that 16:4–31a, the story of Samson and Delilah, which also narrates Samson's death, was not an original part of the story.

This break is also supported by the details of the content of the stories before and after 15:20. In the initial stories of Samson's escapades in chapters 14–15, he gains strength when "the spirit of YHWH rushed upon him" (14:6, 19; 15:14). In contrast, in the story of Samson and the prostitute of Gaza (16:1–3) he is naturally strong, and does not need any additional strength to carry away the city gates. In the story of Samson and Delilah, the phrase "the spirit of YHWH rushed upon him" is lacking, and his strength is connected to his hair. The different underpinnings of these stories suggest that they were written by different people, with different perspectives, and confirm the judgment that 15:20, "He judged Israel during the time of the Philistines for twenty years," was the ending point of an earlier Samson cycle.

Judges 13:2–24 is also an independent unit, telling of Samson's birth. It is an annunciation story (Alter 1983: 115–30; Amit 1999: 292–3) which focuses on Samson's miraculous birth and on his status as a Nazirite. Samson's father, Manoah, is mentioned by name fifteen times in this chapter. It is very striking that he is never mentioned by name in chapters 14–15, which similarly never recognize the role of Samson as a Nazirite, and the connection between his miraculous birth and Nazirite status and his great strength. The messenger of YHWH, who plays such a central role in the chapter, is absent from the following narrative. In addition, 14:4b notes, "at that time, the Philistines were ruling over Israel," offering information that was already known from 13:5, where the messenger of YHWH states "he will begin to save Israel from the hand of the Philistines." Although chapter 13 serves as an introduction in the sense that it introduces Samson, narrating his miraculous birth, it is not an introduction in the sense that it was written with the following material in mind, and introduces the main themes that will follow. These factors are a strong indication that 13:2–24 should be separated as a block from the surrounding material.

Only some minor touching up of the introduction was necessary to help bring these stories together into a cycle; 13:25, "The spirit of YHWH began to stir him in the encampment of Dan, between Zorah and Eshtaol," brilliantly connected the introduction to the rest of the unit, and even beyond. Mention of the "the spirit of YHWH" hints ahead at chapters 14–15, where this spirit (rather than being a Nazirite, or of miraculous birth) is the source of his power. "Between Zorah and Eshtaol" is next mentioned in 16:31, from the last set of stories, where Samson is buried. It is even mentioned in the following story, in 18:2, 8, 11, suggesting that Judg 13:25 not only integrates the introduction to the Samson story into the rest of that story, but into the following story as well. This is confirmed by the mention of the "encampment of Dan," which is also found in 18:12. Thus, 13:25 was written after 13–16, and perhaps even 13–18, had come together,[6] and attempts (successfully) to help tie these disparate chapters together.

There is other likely, but less certain evidence that an editorial hand, or various editorial hands, attempted to smooth together the various units. In several respects Samson's mother plays a very anomalous role at the beginning of chapter 14. She is mentioned in vv. 2, 3, 4, 5, 6, 9, and 16 but then disappears from the narrative. She is absent in vv. 10 and 19, where only his father is mentioned.

Furthermore, her presence at the beginning of the chapter, in connection with Samson's marriage, is quite odd, because typically the father only is involved in such financial transactions. Thus, it is likely that the mother is mentioned at the beginning of chapter 14 as a carryover from chapter 13, where she plays such a significant role. An editor in places added "and his mother" to make the transition between the two chapters smoother. Luckily, as is often the case, this addition was not made in a fully consistent manner, nor is the presence of the groom's mother within a discussion of marital decisions very likely, so the addition may be discerned with some certainty.

In sum, although we lack the type of clear evidence found from the Dead Sea Scrolls concerning the composition of the Gideon cycle, internal evidence makes it quite clear that the Samson material came together from at least three different blocks of material (13:2–24; 14:1–15:19; 16:1–31a). Each unit has different underpinnings and, as I will show, illustrates not only a different part of Samson's life, but has a slightly different take on Samson. An editor or editors probably composed some material to make the individual units work better together as a new whole, creating a more unified Samson Cycle. However, only a partial effort was made in this direction, and the differences between the original building blocks may still be discerned.

The Samson Birth Narrative

As noted by Yair Zakovitch, the Samson birth narrative (13:2–24) has been revised somewhat to fit the Book of Judges. This is clearest from v. 19, "Manoah took the kid and the meal offering and offered them up on the rock to YHWH." The beginning of the chapter, however, nowhere mentions a meal offering in connection to the kid offered to the visitor (v. 15), and the reference to "the rock" is quite confusing, since no rock has been mentioned. These two elements, the meal offering and the rock, are mentioned in Judg 6:18 and 20, where in a scene similar to Judges 13, a messenger of YHWH appears to Gideon. It appears that at some stage of the editing of Judges, various elements from the introduction of the earlier Gideon pericope were transferred to the introduction of the Samson pericope. This was most probably done to help create greater unity and coherence in the book. It is difficult to discern with certainty exactly what the earlier story was, before it was touched up (Zakovitch 1982: 54–8), but the analysis suggested below does not depend on any of these likely secondary elements.

English translations have blurred the fundamental fact that stands behind the chapter – it is the messenger of YHWH who is the father of Samson. This may be seen through a close reading of the text, as well as a comparison of Judges 13 to other annunciation scenes.

V. 3 reads: "The messenger of YHWH appeared to the woman and said to her, 'At this point you are barren and have not given birth; you shall conceive and bear a child.'" V. 5 begins "For you have now conceived and are bearing a child." Both verses use declined forms of הנה, whose main function is to present new information from someone's perspective (Berlin 1983: 91–5). In v. 3, the messenger had just met Manoah's wife, so any information is new to him, justifying the use of הנה. In v. 5, however, truly new information has been given – that the woman who had been barren is now pregnant. This has happened while this divine messenger, and not Manoah, was with Manoah's wife. Furthermore, when Manoah's wife speaks to her husband, she notes (v. 6), "The man of God has come to me"; as noted in the previous chapter, the idiom בא אל is also used in clear sexual contexts, so this may also be translated: "The man of God slept with me." Through this double entendre put in the mouth of the clever wife of Manoah, a double entendre that her dim-witted husband is too stupid to understand, the audience is told of the true father of the "boy to be born."

This reading of chapter 13, suggested by various scholars (Reinhartz 1992: 25–37; Ackerman 1998: 181–207), gains greater credence when Judges 13 is compared to other scenes concerning women who are barren. In 1 Sam 1, for example, Hannah conceives after she prays, but only after (v. 19) "Elkanah was intimate with Hannah his wife, and YHWH remembered her." Rachel is remembered and heeded by God, who opens her womb, in Gen 30:22. Though divine messengers play a significant part in the Genesis narrative, none are present when YHWH remembers Sarah, and she conceives (21:1–2) – a conception which was imagined by her as difficult because both she and her husband were old (18:12).

Judges 13 is totally different from these texts. There is no prayer to God, and no divine remembering. Instead, a divine messenger comes in human form. He is so human that even though the narrator introduces him as a "messenger of YHWH" in v. 3, he is typically called a "*man* of God," a term often used in the Hebrew Bible for a human prophet. He is so human that Manoah cannot recognize that he is really a messenger of YHWH until he disappears and fails to reappear (v. 21).

The parentage of the child explains his superhuman abilities. In many ways, the introduction to the Samson story shares a similar background with Gen 6:1–4 (Hendel 1987: 13–26):

> When men began to increase on earth and daughters were born to them, (2) the divine beings saw how beautiful the daughters of men were and took wives from among those that pleased them. – (3) YHWH said, "My breath shall not abide in man forever, since he too is flesh; let the days allowed him be one hundred and twenty years."- (4) It was then, and later too, that the Nephilim appeared on earth – when the divine beings cohabited with the daughters of men, who bore them offspring. They were the heroes of old, the men of renown.

In both Genesis 6 and here, it is the male angels who lust after human women – the angels are sexual, but have no heavenly female counterparts. Furthermore, in both cases, the children are hybrids of sorts, with supernatural strength (Hendel 1987: 21–3; Coxon 1999: 618–20).

It is likely that the polemical nature of some retellings of Judges 13 in several early post-biblical sources reflects an awareness of the possibility that Samson was the result of angelic conception. Josephus notes both the tremendous beauty of Manoah's wife, which recalls Gen 6:2, and speaks of Manoah's suspicious and jealous nature (Josephus 1968: 5.124–7). Even more remarkable is the tradition in Pseudo-Philo,[7] which opens its retelling with a discussion of whether Manoah or his wife is really the infertile one, a discussion which I believe harks back to a reading of the chapter that suggests that the real reason Mrs. Manoah had not conceived was due to her husband;[7] once impregnated by the messenger of YHWH, she conceived immediately. The retellings reflected in these two texts make more sense if we assume that they are polemical, and the tradition that the angel was the father was still understood in antiquity.

Assuming that the messenger of YHWH was Samson's father might also explain the other main sub-theme of the chapter, the Nazirite vow. This is the only case in the Bible where a Nazirite vow is imposed by anyone outside of the family; elsewhere, it is entered into voluntarily (Num 6:1–21), or is imposed in a vow by the mother (1 Sam 1:11) (Tsevat 1992: 199–204). Yet, in all these cases, a Nazirite is characterized by particular closeness to YHWH. In Num 6:2, the individual wishes "to set himself apart for YHWH." In 1 Sam 1:11, the child "will be given to YHWH for his whole life." The Nazirite is in some senses a non-hereditary priest (Milgrom 1990: 355). The Nazirite's closeness to YHWH is expressed in Numbers 6, most especially through various purity regulations connected to corpse contamination. In Judges 13, these are more severe; like the priest in Lev 22:8 (contrast 17:15), nothing ritually impure may be eaten.

This suggests that Samson's Nazirite status may derive from his parentage. His father is a divine being, and thus Samson must be in the human non-hereditary state closest to being divine, in other words, a Nazirite. This is even intimated in the structure of the text: because Samson's mother has now conceived (from the messenger), the child to be born must be a Nazirite (v. 5). There is nothing in chapter 13 that connects Samson's status as a Nazirite to his strength. He is strong because of his semi-divine father; he is a Nazirite because of his semi-divine father. He is strong due to this parentage, not because of any rituals he might have followed. Phrased differently, there is nothing in chapter 13 to prepare us for chapter 16, where Samson's strength is connected to his (Nazirite) locks. In fact, that chapter really connects Samson's ability to his hair alone (Niditch 1990: 616–17); the connection between his hair and his vow is peripheral there.

It is difficult to determine who wrote this story. Even though it focuses on the Nazirite vow, it was not written by someone from the priestly class. As 1 Samuel 1 and other texts (e.g. Amos 2:11) make clear, not only priests were interested in Nazirites. Furthermore, in its details, the Nazirite prescriptions in Judges differ from those enumerated in Numbers 6.

The main interest of the story is in explaining why Samson had such extraordinary strength, and it suggests that this derived from his true father, who was not Manoah. Such beliefs in angelic conception are not mainstream in ancient Israel, and are reflected elsewhere only in "a mythological fragment" (Hendel 1987: 25) in Genesis 6. I do not mean to suggest that the same individual was responsible for composing both passages. Rather, some group which we can no longer identify was interested in such unions, and believed that such unions took place sporadically. While for them

YHWH's messengers were "very awe-inspiring" (Judg 13:6), they were also physiologically very human, and took an active interest in beautiful women. This folk-belief stands behind the first section of the Samson story.

This belief might intersect with another unusual feature of this text. In general, biblical authors tend to depict males in a more sympathetic light than females (Bird 1997; Bellis 1994). As several scholars have noted, Judges 13 is quite exceptional in this regard. The husband is depicted as a fool, who only realizes that the man of God is a divine messenger after the messenger disappears with the fire of the offering and fails to reappear (v. 21). His wife realized his true nature much earlier, and in contrast to Manoah, saw him at first for what he really was (v. 6): "and his appearance was like the appearance of a divine messenger, very awesome." Manoah's stupidity is emphasized elsewhere in the text as well. He insists on hearing directly what the divine messenger had to say, but the messenger does little more than repeat what he had already said, opening his remarks in a quite condescending fashion (v. 13): "You should be careful concerning everything that I told the woman." Additionally, it is Manoah who makes the stupid mistake of trying to feed a divine being (v. 15), and as noted earlier, only realizes that he had been speaking to a divine messenger very late in the story.

Other features of the text affect the positive characterization of Manoah's wife, and the negative characterization of Manoah. V. 11, "Manoah followed after his wife,"[8] depicts the woman as the leader of her husband, an anomalous situation in biblical texts. In v. 22, Manoah incorrectly thinks that he and his wife will die; his wife corrects him in v. 23. The true etymology of the name Manoah is unknown (see *HALOT* 2.600, s.v. מנוח), but given his behavior, it is easy to characterize him from the root נ(ו)ח, "restful," as "the passive one," perhaps colloquially as even "Mr. Couch Potato." In contrast, Adele Reinhartz has suggested that the anonymity of his wife is due to her close relationship with the divine messenger – through their intimacy, she acquires the anonymous status that typified angels in the pre-exilic period (Reinhartz 1992; 1998: 95–101).

It is notoriously difficult to assign authorship to biblical texts. The past decades have seen this issue get more and more complicated, as we have become less and less certain of the fundamental characteristics of authors whom we call J, E, P or the Deuteronomistic historian. We are less sure of when and where they lived, and exactly what they believed in (Nicholson 1998). Some traditionally early texts are now believed by some to be among the latest in the canon (van Seters, *apud* Nicholson 1998). It is even difficult to broadly say whether a text was written by a man or a woman, and more sophisticated treatments now speak instead of authorship of male and female voices in the text (Brenner and van Dijk-Hemmes 1996).

Relatively few texts reflect a likely female voice and reflect positively on female power. Chapter 13 contrasts with the rest of the Samson stories, which show women as whiny (14:16; 16:15–16), and can be read as stories which warn men of the power of women. It is possible that the positive female voice and the folkloristic background which shares a belief in angelic conception intersect. Perhaps both derive from a circle of female tradents. This would explain why chapter 13 is so anomalous – it does not share the male elite authorship that typifies much of the rest of the Bible.

It is difficult to be more specific about the social location of the text's author. So much is unclear about the structure of ancient Israel, particularly about women's groups, who are poorly reflected in texts (Bird 1997: 81–120). Analogy would suggest that such stories originated on the oral level, but even that is difficult to prove, nor is it clear how this (or any other!) story was changed when it moved from an oral tale to a written text.

It is not, however, totally exceptional that a woman's voice ultimately should become part of the canonical biblical story of Samson. Canonization was a complicated, largely inclusive process that allowed a wide diversity of literature to become incorporated into the biblical text (Davies 1998). This voice is heard elsewhere, most especially in the book of Ruth (Brenner and van Dijk-Hemmes 1996: 105–7; Brenner 1993b: 116–44). What is striking is how very different this voice is from the continuation of the story in chs 14–16, but such diversity is more the rule rather than the exception when a variety of stories are compiled together into a cycle. Judges 13 was most likely chosen to open the cycle because it was the best, most colorful story of Samson's early life available to the editor, and especially with some minor touching-up, it could function as a satisfactory introduction. Given that we do not know what alternatives, if any, the editor rejected in composing this cycle, there is little more we can say about the reason why chapter 13, despite its anomalies, opens this cycle.

Samson and the Timnite Woman

With the first verse of chapter 14, we move from one anonymous woman – Samson's mother, to another – the Timnite woman who (v. 3) "is right in his [Samson's] eyes." This unit is comprised of a loosely connected set of stories which illustrate Samson's single-handed superiority over the Philistines. Yet, the key to the real theme and background of this group of stories is already in the story's introduction. Samson's interest in this woman is no ordinary desire or lust; rather (v. 4), "His father and mother did not realize that this was YHWH's doing: He [YHWH] was seeking a pretext against the Philistines."

This theme and others connected to it help to organize the stories in 14–15 into a coherent whole which distinguishes it from what precedes and follows. It is not clear that all of the stories in these two chapters originated from the same person or even from the same narrow circle. The fight over the Timnite woman motivates many of the stories, but she has disappeared as a factor by the end of chapter 15. Chapter 14 has the play between the roots ירד, "to descend," and רדה/ה, "to take honey out of a beehive" as its underpinning (14:1–10, 19). In contrast, the first part of chapter 15 is characterized by the *Leitwort* עשׂה/ה (15:3–11). In all but the last story, the numbers are almost all multiples of three: thirty companions (14:11), thirty articles of clothing (14:12–13), three days (14:14), thirty slain people (14:19) and three hundred foxes (15:4).[9] The end of the chapter breaks this pattern when Samson is tied up with two new ropes (15:13) and goes on to slay one thousand people (15:15). In general, the end of the story, with its strong theological coloring (15:18) and its strong etiological interests (15:17, 19) does not fully cohere with what precedes it. This suggests, not surprisingly, that chapters 14–15 do not have a totally straightforward history. They might incorporate a variety of stories from different oral traditions, and/or might have been touched up and edited after they initially came together. Nevertheless, especially when put into the broader framework of Judges 13–16, and compared to what precedes and follows, chapters 14–15 do cohere.

The stories gathered together in 14–15, in contrast to the rest of the Samson material, have very close affinities to wisdom material and themes. As alluded to above, the introduction to the material, specifically 14:4, "His father and mother did not realize that this was YHWH's doing: He [YHWH] was seeking a pretext against the Philistines," offers an important clue concerning the context of the unit. This idea, that YHWH is really in control, even when people appear to be acting of their own volition, characterizes wisdom literature (Murphy 1992: 920–31). This is the main theme of Qohelet, which emphasizes in great detail YHWH's control, most especially in the famous chapter 3, which states that the cycles are all directed by God, and humans might try to understand the way they work, but to no avail (3:10–11). Several proverbs in Proverbs make a similar point; for example, Prov 19:21, "Many designs are in a man's mind, but it is YHWH's plan that is accomplished." This idea, however, is not unique to pure wisdom contexts; for example, the Joseph story, which has been influenced by wisdom ideas, but is not itself a wisdom story, has Joseph say to his brothers after their father has died (Gen 50:20), "Besides, although you intended me harm, God intended it for good, so as to bring about the present result – the survival of many people" (von Rad 1976: 439–47).

Judges 14–15 show at least as broad an influence of wisdom as the Joseph cycle (Crenshaw 1976: 429–94; Gordon 1995: 94–105). Riddles are found in 14, 18a and 18b, and are a crucial theme of chapter 14. Eight of the seventeen occurrences of the word חידה, "riddle," in the entire Bible are in this chapter! According to Prov 1:6, from the introduction of the book, one of the goals of the book is "For understanding proverb and epigram, the words of the wise and their riddles (וחידתם)," and the numerical sayings in Proverbs 30 may have originated as riddles. It is striking that the three riddles in Judges 14 are all in poetic parallelism, a form which characterizes the learned book of Proverbs, but most likely did not characterize popular Israelite riddles. Thus, the thematic significance of riddles further ties this unit to wisdom traditions.

As a result of the rising interest in the last part of the twentieth century in both wisdom literature and women in biblical scholarship, Proverbs 1–9, with its depiction of the dangers of the strange or foreign women, have been highlighted (Blenkinsopp 1991; Camp 1981; 1985; 1987; Newsom 1989). This is also a theme of Judges 14–15. In contrast to Judges 16, Samson's interest in the Timnite woman not only endangers himself, but has broader ramifications when the Philistines encamp to fight Judah (15:9). It is only in chapters 14–15, but not in 16, where the Philistines are called by the highly derogatory out-group label "the uncircumcised ones" (14:3; 15:18), which emphasizes their role as outsiders or foreigners (Niditch 1990: 608–24, esp. 621–4). Perhaps the anonymity of the woman in these chapters, in distinction to Delilah in chapter 16, helps to equate her with the anonymous, archetypal foreigner (זרה or נכריה) of Proverbs 1–9. In fact, the Timnite woman is like the woman of Qoh 7:26, created especially to ensnare men (Rudman 1997).

Chapters 14–15 recall wisdom themes and statements in other ways as well. Wisdom literature is very interested in cause and effect, especially in the form of talion (von Rad 1972: 124–37). Thus, Judg 15:10b, where the Philistines say, "We have come to take Samson prisoner, and to do to him as he did to us" and 11b, where Samson says, "as they did to me, so I did to them," are very wisdom-like. In fact, the same idea is explored, using the same language (note the identical doubling of the verb עשׂה/ה) in Prov 24:29: "Do not say, 'I will do to him what he did to me; I will pay the man what he deserves.'"

Even the episode where Samson asks the Judeans to tie him up, with the expectation that God will come to his rescue, might echo a wisdom text. One strain in Proverbs emphasizes the worthlessness of human power in a world controlled by YHWH (Prov 21:31): "The horse is readied for the day of battle, but victory comes from YHWH."[10] That Samson's victory "comes from YHWH" is made very clear from 15:14, "When he reached Lehi, the Philistines came shouting to meet him. Thereupon the spirit of YHWH gripped him, and the ropes on his arms became like flax that catches fire; the bonds melted off his hands," and is further emphasized by the highly theological conclusion to chapter 15.

Wisdom influence on this section, or at least a strong wisdom background for this section's author or editor, explains several other details of the text. The beginning of chapter 14 emphasizes Samson's strong sense of responsibility to his parents; this is a frequent wisdom theme, developed already in the first chapter of Proverbs (1:8). In 14:13, the Philistines are promised thirty pieces of clothing (סדינים) if they can answer the riddle. סדינים is a rare word, found only twice more in the Bible; one of these is in Prov 31:24. The root used in Judg 14:15, פתה/ה, "to entice," is particularly frequent in Proverbs, where פתי is the typical word for the fool. The use of the unusual word מרע for "companion" four times in chapters 14 and 15 is unexpected; two of the word's other four occurrences are in Proverbs and Job. Though no one of these themes or roots is unique to wisdom contexts, they are more frequent in wisdom than in other contexts, and their use together here betrays likely wisdom background or influence.

It is even possible that Prov 6:29 may stand behind the depiction of the Timnite woman's father's refusal to let Samson see her.

The similarities between these two texts are highlighted through italics:

> Prov 6:29: "It is the same with one who *sleeps with* his fellow's *wife*; None who touches her will go *unpunished* (ינקה)."

> Judg 15:1–3: "Some time later, in the season of the wheat harvest, Samson came to visit his *wife*, bringing a kid as a gift. He said, 'Let me *sleep with* my *wife* in the chamber' but her father would not let him go in. (2) 'I was sure,' said her father, 'that you had taken a dislike to her, so I gave her to your wedding *companion*. But her younger sister is more beautiful than she; let her become your wife instead.' (3) Thereupon Samson declared, 'Now the Philistines *can have no claim* (ינקה) against me for the harm I shall do them."

Once juxtaposed, Judges 15 can be read as an ironic unfolding of the admonition in Prov 6:29.

Judges 14–15 should be read in much the same way as many of the sections in Proverbs 1–9, which provide several illustrative tales of the danger of the foreign woman. The two types of story-tellings are not identical – in Proverbs 1–9, the characters are anonymous, and no historical setting is offered, in contrast to the escapades of Samson with the Philistines set in the pre-monarchic period. Thus, Judges 14–15 should be read as historicized-wisdom[11] in the way that some scholars want to read Esther or the Joseph story (Talmon 1963). Thus, there is a range of ways in which authors/scholars affiliated with wisdom schools might teach their lessons concerning foreign women: some would use short, two-part proverbs (e.g. Prov 23: 27), others favored illustrative examples of nameless women (e.g. Proverbs 7), while still others preferred stories with named characters set in a historical period.

In that sense, the extant biblical wisdom text that is closest to Judges 14–15 is the framework of Job. I imagine that the author of the Judges material, like the author of the Job framework, knew traditional stories about his hero. (Ezekiel 14:14, 20 indicates that Job was widely known.) He took these stories and re-framed them into his own world-view to express the lessons that he wanted to illustrate. In the case of Samson, the wisdom scholar likely had before him (1) material concerning the foreign woman; (2) material concerning the mysterious ways of YHWH; and (3) material concerning talionic behavior. He wove these themes into stories he knew, probably reshaping them significantly and perhaps creating new ones as well, creating the historicized tale we now have in chapters 14–15.

This wisdom perspective is missing from chapter 13, and as we shall see, from chapter 16 as well. In fact, it is difficult to imagine that a wisdom scholar could have depicted a woman in the manner that Manoah's wife is portrayed in chapter 13; her depiction contrasts sharply with Job's wife, whose main function is to act as a foil for her husband as she says (Job 2:9), "curse God and drop dead!"[12] Unfortunately, because most scholars have not begun by isolating each of the components of the Samson story from the other, they have not noted sufficiently how only 14–15 are so wisdom-like.

As I noted earlier, all stories, including this one, are complex. By this analysis, which emphasizes wisdom to the exclusion of other elements, I do not mean to suggest that this is "pure wisdom," whatever that might mean. As I noted above, it is likely that other traditional material, especially concerning Samson as a strong man, a Heracles-like figure, was borrowed from traditional material and reshaped (Margalith 1985; 1986a; 1986b; 1987). The etiologies at the end of chapter 15 do not typify wisdom texts. I return to the purpose of this study – to understand, to the extent possible, how, why, when, and by whom these stories were written. I believe that offering a wisdom background for the core of chapters 14–15 is the most satisfactory suggestion in that regard.

The Death of Samson

As noted earlier, chapter 16 is a late addition to the Samson cycle, as indicated by the ending formula in 15:20, "He judged Israel during the time of the Philistines for twenty years." In 16:4–31, the story of Samson and Delilah is placed where it is because it is a story that explains the death of the super-strong Samson; hence it must come at the conclusion of the cycle. It is unclear if 16:1–3, the story of Samson and the prostitute from Gaza, should be seen as a story separate from 16:4ff., or is part of the same story.

Such simple issues as the connection of 16:1–3 to what follows will remain unresolved until we can find some way of determining (1) how much unity a particular story must have, and (2) how we might know if particular formulae are editorial or authorial. These verses certainly *may* be read as a separate, self-contained unit.

However, this does not imply that they *are* a separate composition, because often a text can be pulled out of a larger unit and read as a self-contained whole even if it was not written as such. It is clearly differentiated from what precedes because Samson does not need the spirit of YHWH to descend upon him in order to perform supernatural feats of strength.

Like 16:4ff., 16:1–3 is centered on Samson's relations with a woman. This shorter unit also focuses on Samson's ability to use his great strength to destroy a man-made structure, which he accomplishes by seizing something crucial (Hebrew אחז in vv. 3 and 21). In both parts of chapter 16, the Philistines lie in ambush (Hebrew ארב) for him (vv. 2, 9, 12). The first story begins, and the second ends, in Gaza (1, 21).

However, there are significant differences between the two units. The first is shorter, and the dialogue which characterizes the second unit is totally lacking. In the first, the woman is nameless; in the second she is named. The first looks like a type of etiological tale, explaining why there is a strange city gate out of context in Hebron; the second has no such function. On balance, the differences seem to outnumber the similarities, but I am uncertain if they are decisive enough to ascertain that we are dealing with separate compositional units, especially given the thematic similarities between the two. Or do we say instead that either these thematic similarities caused 16:1–3 to become attracted to 16:4ff., or that certain themes naturally migrated between these two stories, making them fit together better?

The evidence of the formula opening 16:4, "some time later," is somewhat ambiguous. Some scholars have claimed that this is "a common editorial phrase connecting independent narratives; it carries no chronological significance…" (Cogan and Tadmor 1988: 78) and in *most* cases the phrase seems to be used this way. Yet, it is also used at least once within a single story written by a single author to indicate passage of time in a narrative.[13] Furthermore, the origin of the phrase as an editorial device most likely derives from its use as a compositional device. Thus, although statistics suggest that the phrase is typically used editorially, these have no bearing on its use in any particular case.

Perhaps one day more work will be done on the structure of the biblical story that will bear some fruit on whether 16:1–3 should be read as a separate unit, or should be read as the introduction of a longer unit, foreshadowing what follows. Certainly, if it is read independently, the four units which then comprised the Samson cycle would be extremely imbalanced in size, but we do not yet know if the ancient Israelites had the same sense of balance that we do. Nor do we know if such cycles were more often presented in three or four scenes. It would seem that the evidence of Jonah and Ruth suggests that four-scene stories were more typical (Magonet 1992: 937–8), though the evidence of Ruth is somewhat ambiguous, and might favor a three-scene story.[14] In sum, more extensive basic research on the structure of biblical stories, the overlap between phrases used editorially and compositionally, and the amount of thematic, verbal and stylistic similarity expected in a composition by a single author might help resolve the issue of whether or not Judg 16:1–3 should be connected to, or separated from, what follows. However, all of these are complex questions, each deserving a monograph, and they cannot be resolved here in order to clarify the status of 16:1–3.

In many ways, 16:4ff. differ from chapters 13–15, reinforcing the judgment about 15:20 ending the original cycle, and making it clear that this is a composition by a different author. The folktale nature of chapter 13 and the positive power it offers to women is absent in chapter 16. The wisdom terminology and ideas found in 14–15 are absent as well. In contrast to the previous sections, chapter 16:4ff. has a named Philistine woman. In terms of distinguishing the units, it does not matter that Delilah might very well be a symbolic name meaning "dangling hair" or "flirt" (*HALOT* 1.222, s.v. דלילה); the women in the other chapters are unnamed in any way. The Philistine governors (סרנים) appear in this unit for the first time. Finally, unlike the previous unit, Samson's strength derives only from his hair (16:19); the spirit of YHWH does not provide this power.

Rhetorically, a big chunk of this unit is also fundamentally different than the earlier units. 16:6–20 uses the common biblical three-four pattern to describe how Delilah tries to discover the source of Samson's power; she fails the first three times, and succeeds on the fourth (Zakovitch 1978). This section is typified by repetition with variation as it leads up to the climax, where Samson reveals his secret. A similar style, on a smaller scale, is seen in Jotham's parable in 9:7–15. This style is fundamentally different from what precedes – it is neither folkloristic like chapter 13, nor typical of wisdom like chapters 14–15. Unfortunately, it is difficult to place this type of narrative more specifically within ancient Israelite culture, specifying who might have told or listened to this style.

In terms of theme and content, however, this section of chapter 16 has clear affinities to other biblical material.

> The act is meant to be a testimony to the superiority of the Philistine god over the Israelite God. But the Philistines have misread what is happening, and by the time this episode is over, their victory has turned into a devastating defeat, first of their god and secondly of the people.
>
> (P.D. Miller and Roberts 1977: 67)

This comment by Miller and Roberts on the ark narrative in 1 Samuel, specifically on the competition between YHWH and Dagon in 1 Samuel 5, fits exactly our unit, which may be called "Yahweh *versus* the gods of Canaan" (Wharton 1973: 62). Indeed, outside of the use of Dagon in place names and a reference in Chronicles that depends on 1 Samuel 5, Judg 16:23 is the only verse outside of 1 Samuel 15 to mention this deity. The major question of the ark narrative is "who is supreme, who is God: Yahweh or Dagon?" (P.D. Miller and Roberts 1977: 73). This is raised explicitly in the repetition in vv. 23 and 24, where the Philistines first say (v. 23), "Our god has delivered into our hands our enemy Samson" and then the narrative continues (v. 24), "When the people saw him, they sang praises to their god, chanting, 'Our god has delivered into our hands the enemy who devastated our land, and who slew so many of us.'" This final scene is set in the Dagon Temple, and it is there that Samson prays. This prayer is introduced by the narrator with the mention of YHWH, and contains references (in a single verse, v. 28) to both LORD YHWH and God. It is efficacious; the fact that (30b) "Those who were slain by him as he died outnumbered those who had been slain by him when he lived" shows the absolute power of YHWH over Dagon. As in the ark narrative, "the Philistines have misread what is happening," and have not realized that the only reason Samson was brought to their temple was to destroy it, indicating the ultimate superiority of YHWH.

This final unit is thus theological in a way that fundamentally differs from the previous units. As noted, it is similar to sections of the ark narrative, as well as to other biblical passages such as 2 Kgs 18:17–19:37 which emphasize the superiority of YHWH over the gods of Assyria. This theme is barely visible in chapter 13, and is also absent in chapters 14–15, where no Philistine deities are mentioned and the battle is between Samson and the Philistines, though YHWH does come to Samson's aid against the Philistine *people*.

The motif of "my God is better than your god(s)" is so common in the Bible that we cannot posit a single *Sitz im Leben* for it. The most we can say is that the author of (this section of) chapter 16 wrote in a more structured fashion than the other authors, and had a more explicit theological agenda – his focus is as much on YHWH as it is on Samson, and his writing style was more structured than the previous pericopae. Kathryn Kravitz has made the tantalizing suggestion that the reference to Samson's blindness is an allusion to the blinding of Zedekiah in 2 Kgs 25:7 (Kravitz 1999: 162). The fact that the uncommon phrase "bound him in fetters" is used in both contexts (Judg 16:21, 2 Kgs 25:7) might be sufficient to buttress this claim. If correct, then the function of this final unit may be contextualized historically, and contrasted even more sharply with the previous units. This unit is meant as consolation, suggesting that the blinding and killing of Zedekiah (=Samson) will soon bring death to the Babylonians and ultimate restoration to Israel.[15] The destruction of YHWH's temple is displaced to the destruction of Dagon's temple along with those celebrating there. YHWH does to Israel's enemies what he had done to Judah (Lam 1:22); perhaps the time has come to restore Israel's days as of old (Lam 5:21).

The Samson Cycle as a Whole

The previous sections make it abundantly clear that Judges 13–16 have a complex history, and derive from various sources which have been combined. Even though each unit has a different structure, and makes a different point, in various ways the units do fit together. Some of this was shown above, in noting how chapter 13 in some ways functions as a proper introduction to the cycle as a whole. Other features create a sense of coherence as well. The Timnite woman, especially in her whiny behavior, anticipates Delilah. The number three thousand appears in both 15:11 and 16:27. Prayer plays a significant role at the end of both chapters 15 and 16 (Exum 1983: 3–45).[16] The attempt of the Judeans to control Samson by tying him with new ropes (15:13) foreshadows Delilah's actions in the following chapter (see esp. 16:11–12). Both chapters 14 and 16 open in a similar fashion, with Samson going somewhere and seeing a woman. Given the fact that these stories have separate origins, it is possible that these similarities are coincidental. More likely, given their extent, they are not coincidental, but were created after the stories were combined together. Perhaps elements naturally moved from one story to another; alternatively, they were transferred intentionally by an editor to create a more homogeneous cycle.

How then are we to read the cycle in its entirety? It is best to investigate this issue by looking at other attempts at interpreting the Samson cycle.

Several earlier scholars saw the broken Nazirite vow as the main thematic element of the story (Blenkinsopp 1963; Crenshaw 1978). This theme, however, is central only in chapter 13. It appears only once in chapter 16, when Samson tells Delilah (v. 17), "No razor has ever touched my head, for I have been a Nazirite to God since I was in my mother's womb. If my hair were cut, my strength would leave me and I should become as weak as an ordinary man." It is totally absent from chapters 14–15. Though some believe that these chapters implicitly narrate the various ways that Samson breaks his vows – drinking wine at parties, becoming impure through corpse contamination – this is in no way marked in the text. Had an editor wished to create a larger unity with the Nazirite vow as its central theme, it would have been easy to add a few words in chapters 14–15 to make this theme clearer.

It is not surprising that various attempts at finding structural arguments for the coherence of the Samson material have also been advocated (Exum 1981). Such patterns suffer from the same problems noted in Chapter Two concerning Fokkelman's suggested structure(s) for Gen 11:1–9. Common words are used in creating parallels, the sections created are not really balanced in terms of length, features that might interfere with the proposed structure are ignored, and an inordinately complex structure that could not have been conceived by the author–editor is constructed. For these reasons, such undertakings must be rejected.

Others have suggested broad categories which tie the chapter together, such as reading 13–16 as an "epic" offering "a fine extended example of story-telling in the traditional mode" (Niditch 1990: 608). Such suggestions ignore the fact that parts of the cycle reflect wisdom influence, and thus are not traditional. In addition, the discovery of different folkloristic motifs in each of the sections is not sufficient to make the whole cohere.

These suggestions for *the* theme of the Samson story are not successful because each ignores the fact that the cycle has a complex history, in which at least three different stories have been blended together. Especially given that there are various indications of an editor's hand to smooth out the transition between these stories or episodes, it is particularly appropriate to see what might tie them together. But they cannot be put into a straightjacket in this process.

Thematically, and in terms of the social location in ancient Israel that the author came from, these stories could not fit neatly together without radical revision. The Nazirite vows which are so important in chapter 13 would need to be repeated and form a clear skeleton throughout. The editor would need to decide how Samson's Nazirite status, birth from an angelic father, long hair, and sudden possession with the spirit of YHWH all fit together, and would have had to modify the stories accordingly. He might have smoothed out minor stylistic differences as well, such as those between stories with unnamed female protagonists, and chapter 16, with Delilah.

We can only surmise that the types of changes that are called for to create a truly coherent cycle went beyond what a biblical redactor would typically do. Instead, stories were brought together in chronological order; this is the major factor that allows these originally separate stories to cohere somewhat. In the earliest stage of the cycle, a birth story (chapter 13) was followed by the stories of the exploits of the mature Samson (chapters 14–15). When material concerning the death of Samson became available for inclusion in the book (chapter 16), it was added at the end. Without knowing what additional material, if any, might have been available to the editor which he opted not to include, we cannot decide what the criteria for inclusion or exclusion might have been.

Thus, the Samson cycle represents a model of redaction that is weak from a thematic and stylistic perspective: ultimately, centrifugal forces are greater than centripetal ones. It is similar to the loose editing of the prophetic cycles of Elijah or Elisha, which also incorporate diverse material from different time periods and genres (Rofé 1988). Only a complete investigation of the other cycles in Judges will indicate if the final form of Judges 13–16 is the norm or the exception. However, given the current climate of biblical studies, where meaning is often found in secondarily composed units at the expense of the integrity of the individual building blocks of these units, the ultimate form of the Samson pericope is an important reminder that sometimes different types of material come together for a variety of reasons, and we must be careful not to ignore the history of the unit's composition when considering it as a whole. We cannot always impose *our* desire to find order and coherence on ancient texts.

5

POETRY AND PROSE IN
JUDGES 4–5

It is extremely difficult to say anything new about Judges 4–5. These two chapters form a unique unit in Judges. They are not a short story – chapters 4 and 5 are clearly two different units, composed by (at least) two different people. Yet they are not a cycle in the usual sense either. As we saw with the Samson material, a cycle is composed of a series of shorter blocks of material, which are edited to form a series of narratives in chronological order about a judge. Though Judges 5 presents itself as subsequent to Judges 4, as a victory song celebrating the defeat of the Canaanites narrated in chapter 4, the bulk of chapter 5 is really a poetic variant of chapter 4. Unlike the cycles, the events told in the two chapters are simultaneous, rather than subsequent.

This of course is not the only such pairing of simultaneous events told twice, first in prose, then in poetry (Watts 1992; Weitzman 1997). Exodus 14 and 15 are the best-known example of this phenomenon. Given that the Song of the Sea in Exodus, like Judges 5, is also typically considered to be archaic biblical poetry, Exodus 14–15 will often be an important reference point for evaluating Judges 4–5.

This chapter will consider three issues concerning Judges 4–5. The first is a classic issue of biblical studies, which nevertheless needs further exploration: the use of Judges 5 by the modern historian of ancient Israel. I will argue that most scholars have not paid sufficient attention to the issue of genre in exploring this question. I will then explore the more recent suggestion by Baruch Halpern that the prose account in Judges 4 was created through a (mis)interpretation of the poetic Judges 5. For several reasons, this is an important thesis, which deserves careful examination. It raises the issue of the extent to which Israelite historians were motivated by what Halpern calls "antiquarian interest." It also suggests that some of the types of close interpretation associated with the rabbis might actually have their origins much earlier, already in the (pre-exilic) biblical period. Finally, having explored certain aspects of chapters 4 and 5 separately, I will briefly engage what might be considered part of the canonical criticism: why have both chapters 4 and 5 been preserved by the historian(s) responsible for Judges?

Judges 5 and the Historian

The dominant position concerning the Song of Deborah and Judges 5 was articulated over one hundred years ago in the International Critical Commentary on Judges by George F. Moore (Moore 1895); he saw the poem as "a triumphal ode," and suggested that "by the vividness of every touch, and especially by the elevation and intensity of feeling which pervades it, it makes the impression of having been written by one who witnessed the great events it commemorates" (Moore 1895: 107). He notes that:

> Critics have been almost unanimous in attributing the Ode to a contemporary, and a participant in the glorious struggle it celebrates. So, to make but a single quotation, Kuenen writes, "Form and contents alike prove that it is rightly ascribed by all competent judges to a contemporary."
>
> (Moore 1895: 129)

Throughout, it creates an "impression of reality," and its historical representations "agree entirely with the historical situation, so far as we are able from our very scanty materials to reconstruct it" (Moore 1895: 131). In sum, "It [the Song of Deborah] is the oldest extant monument of Hebrew literature, and the only contemporaneous monument of Hebrew history before the foundation of the kingdom" (Moore 1895: 132–3).

The three key points of Moore – the early date of Judges 5, the suggestion of its genre as a victory ode or poem, and the insistence that it may be used in a straightforward fashion by the modern historian of ancient Israel, have found widespread, though not total assent among biblical scholars.

Moore's least controversial assertion concerns the early date of the poem. In 1936, Albright claimed that "Nearly all competent biblical scholars believe that the Song of Deborah is the oldest document which the Bible has preserved in approximately its original form" (Albright 1936: 26). In 1969, Peter Craigie introduced a comparative Assyrian example to similarly suggest that the song is "a very ancient text" (Craigie 1969: 254). That same year, A.D.H. Mayes noted that the archaeological evidence used to posit a twelfth century date is faulty, and suggested that the events narrated are from the eleventh rather than the twelfth century (Mayes 1969: 353–60), still very ancient by the standards of biblical scholarship. Thus, a 1974 study could conclude that "The inescapable conclusion that emerges from a comparative study is that there is nothing in Judges 5 that could not have been written during the twelfth or eleventh century B.C." (Globe 1974: 497).

A 1975 study by D.N. Freedman, one of the key figures studying early biblical poetry, shows a surprising similarity with the observations of Moore, nearly a century earlier: In reference to both Exodus 15 and Judges 5, he speaks of the "growing consensus about their early date" (Freedman 1980: 131), and suggests that they were composed by "primary witnesses to those events" (Freedman 1980: 132) "to celebrate recent decisive victories" (Freedman 1980: 149). He "believe[s] that the song of Deborah reflects the actual state of affairs at that time" (Freedman 1980: 153), namely the twelfth century (Freedman 1980: 152). His conclusion is similar to that of Moore:"Essentially, the poems taken together confirm the historicity of key events" (Freedman 1980: 160).

More recently, archaeologists have tried to fill in the details of the poem with studies of the social aspects of ancient life which are better understood as a result of close archaeological analysis. This is clearest in the work of Lawrence E. Stager. He notes that "The antiquity of the Song of Deborah is not in doubt: it was composed in the 12th or, at the latest, 11th century B.C." (Stager 1986: 224). Yet, unlike many earlier scholars, he does not want to assert that it is a true eyewitness account, and notes:

> Regardless of their historicity, for the past events of the Song of Deborah to ring true, the poet must have passed the test of verisimilitude, having grounded his story in setting and circumstance that seemed plausible to his contemporary audience.
>
> (Stager 1986: 224)

He then goes on to offer a very plausible suggestion for why particular tribes might not have participated in the battle, based on the tribes' geographical locations and likely means of subsistence. His thesis takes as its starting point the basic historicity of vv. 14–18.

The 1993 article of J. David Schloen builds upon Stager, and is methodologically similar to it. He too assumes "that the Song is one of the oldest compositions preserved in the Hebrew Bible" (Schloen 1993: 20) and notes that "More difficult to establish is the poem's historicity. It is hard to believe that it does not celebrate an actual battle, but there is no way of demonstrating its accuracy in detail" (Schloen 1993: 20–1). Yet, he accepts the basic outlines of the poem, and posits a "caravan hypothesis," that the major motivation for the *real war* described here is the disruption caused to Israelite and Midianite caravan traders (Schloen 1993: 18–38).

Stager and Schloen have presented theories. They both depend on relatively early dating of the Song. Certainly, they represent an advance, in that they have moved away from an eyewitness mode to a more sophisticated type of analysis, suggesting that the poem needs to make sense in its context, which might be removed somewhat from the original events themselves. Yet, they have taken for granted the early date of the poem, and have done little to advance the question of the poem's genre.

The three assumptions shared by Moore, Freedman, and a majority of biblical scholars concerning the date of the song, its genre, and how the song might be used by the contemporary historian, continue to inform biblical scholarship. Yet, these assumptions deserve further study. The assumptions will be examined in that order, since the issues of date and genre are primary questions which need to be investigated before we can decide how a historian might use this chapter.

As Mayes correctly noted, there is no archeological evidence that bears on the dating of this chapter. There is, however, linguistic evidence. Especially after the discovery of Ugaritic, a datable corpus that predates the Hebrew Bible, it is possible to compare the language used in the archaic biblical corpus to Ugaritic texts, to see the number of non-standard BH features that this corpus preserves that are related to these earlier texts. This type of investigation was carried out initially by Albright, and continued with his students and their students. The most detailed work was by David A. Robertson, who concluded that Exodus 15 is older than Judges 5, and that Judges 5 has a substantial number of standard, non-archaic features. He notes that this means that it should be dated between the twelfth and eighth centuries, and he favors a date in the early part of this period, though he does so very tentatively (Robertson 1972: 153–6; Goodwin 1969).

But not all concur. The greatest dissent comes from Michael Waltisberg who, based on various Aramaisms in the Song, concludes that it derives from the fifth to the third century (Waltisberg 1999). Many of these possible Aramaisms were noted earlier; C.F. Burney in 1918 called them "a natural phenomenon," and felt that they did not imply a late date (Burney 1970: 176). Other scholars have been aware of the possibility that the archaic features of Judges 5 might really be archaisms rather than true archaic language, and have suggested various reasons why the former possibility is unlikely (Globe 1974: 509–11). Given the number of unusual linguistic features which do match pre-Israelite northwest Semitic inscriptions, the various arguments for an early date advanced by Robertson and others carry certain weight. Yet, the dialect of the poem is far from uniform, and does not consistently represent what scholars construct at the earliest phase of BH. The majority of the poem is in standard biblical Hebrew (SBH), and it may even contain some later elements (Kutscher 1982: 12). Thus, there is no linguistic evidence that the poem *as it is now preserved* dates from the period of these events themselves.

We do not know when these events happened or if they happened, so we cannot decide how close the earliest language of the poem is to these events. The dating of archaic biblical poetry cannot be accomplished with great precision. Finally, there are indications that the poem continued to develop. Like other biblical texts, it did not fossilize. Its language changed as it was transmitted, and there is every reason to believe that large and small changes to its content transpired as well (Caquot 1986).

In closing the investigation of the dating of Judges 5, it is crucial to note that there are no external historical documents which bear on the events narrated in the chapter. Thus, the statement of Moore, that its historical representations "agree entirely with the historical situation, so far as we are able from our very scanty materials to reconstruct it," mirrored in Freedman's claim that the poem may "confirm the historicity of key events," is meaningless. Judges 5 is not comparable, for example, to the way that the account of Sennacherib's third campaign, an external, non-biblical, primary piece of evidence, confirms pieces of 2 Kgs 18:13–14 (Cogan and Tadmor 1988: 246–51); there is no outside evidence that directly bears on the veracity of Judges 5.

Most significantly, there has been some movement away from the notion that Judges 5 is an eyewitness account of the events it depicts. This is important; though even eyewitness accounts clearly have their biases, there *can be* a *broad* correlation between the closeness of an account to the event that it narrates and its accuracy. Within the world of modern biblical scholarship, Peter R. Ackroyd voiced an important caution as early as 1952, when he suggested that the Song was similar to the medieval tales of kings, which continue to develop as they are retold (Ackroyd 1952: 160–2). The iconoclastic G.W. Ahlström could speak of "The poet, who probably composed this work long after the historical event it celebrates" (Ahlström 1977: 288). Michael D. Coogan, picking up the theme of Ackroyd, also points to the problems that the broad genre represents for the historian. Quoting C. Bowra, he notes that "poetry, especially heroic poetry, is a poor substitute for history." Therefore "we will not attempt to answer the many historical questions which have been asked with reference to Judges 5; most of these questions are unanswerable because of the nature of the evidence" (Coogan 1978: 143). For this reason, "specific historical conclusions cannot be drawn from it" (Coogan 1978: 144).

These suggestions raise the issue of genre, which along with date, is the central issue for the modern historian using ancient sources. Without any question, the broad genre of the poem is poetry. This too has implications for its use in reconstructing history. This was most clearly noted over half a century ago by Gillis Gerleman, though his advice has been largely ignored. He notes that the song is characterized by "impressionistic snapshots" (Gerleman 1951: 172) and "paratactic, atomizing technique, logical relationships being almost completely eliminated" (Gerleman 1951: 171). "Instead of logical coherence, in which one event follows another consequently, this impressionistic poetry works by contrasts" (Gerleman 1951: 172). These observations, which some others have further buttressed (Coogan 1978; Ahlström 1977; Hauser 1980), suggest that the broad genre of the poem presents certain insurmountable problems for the modern historian who might want to use it for reconstructing ancient history. Judges 5 is poetic – it is not a straightforward narrative recounting, where "all" we need to do is determine the historian's bias. Instead, it is poetry, and aesthetic elements may override historical ones, and the paratactic style cannot easily be shoehorned into a straightforward chronological reconstruction of what the author believed happened.

Usually genre labels are more narrow than "poetry" or "prose." Thus, typically the Song has been considered "a victory poem." This position has been part of critical scholarship from at least the time of Moore, who called it "a triumphal ode," and is certainly the majority position. If we could develop some understanding of this genre, we would be able to better appreciate how the Song might be used by the historian. Unfortunately, this is impossible.

The most detailed attempt at discussing the form-critical genre is by Alan J. Hauser. He is conscious of the problem of asserting that both Exodus 15 and Judges 5 should be considered together as "songs of victory," including the fact that they do not agree stylistically with clearly marked songs of victory, such as 1 Sam 18:6–7:

> When the troops came home and David returned from killing the Philistine, the women of all the towns of Israel came out singing and dancing to greet King Saul with timbrels, shouting, and sistrums. The women sang as they danced, and they chanted:Saul has slain his thousands; David, his tens of thousands!

To my mind, the fact that Judges 5 is so very different from this certain "victory song" should make us extremely cautious about claiming that it is a victory song. Yet, Hauser plows ahead, developing a five-part structure for the "victory song." Some of his form-critical criteria, such as "the use of the divine name," are overly broad. It is difficult to believe that others, such as "the water motif," appeared in all victory songs, rather than happening to be in both Exodus 15 and Judges 5, and in any case, water is certainly not as significant in Judges 5 as it is in Exodus 15. Hauser notes that a comparison of both poems highlights "diversity within commonality" (Hauser 1987: 281). To my mind, the diversity significantly outweighs the commonality. In addition, even if both poems do share significant form-critical similarities, Hauser brings no evidence which shows that these similarities suggest that they should both be classified as victory songs.

A minority of scholars has considered the Song to be a liturgy. This position was first articulated by the noted Psalms scholar, Artur Weiser, and has been adopted by John Gray (Weiser 1959; Gray 1977; 1988). They both then connect this poem to the fall enthronement festival. Modern scholarship now tends to de-emphasize this festival, and certainly does not follow the excesses of Sigmund Mowinckel, who connected much, if not most of the biblical liturgical material to this putative festival. Thus, rather than exploring the narrow position associating Judges 5 with that festival, it is worth exploring the broader position that it is a liturgical text of sorts.

Initially, this is a very attractive position, because there are significant elements that seem liturgical in the Song. As early as 1922, Albright called "bless YHWH" in vv. 2 and 9 a "liturgical phrase" (Albright 1922: 74 n. 2). The phrase appears with "to bless" as a passive participle (ברוך) nine times in Psalms,[1] and the identical imperative (ברכו) is found three times in Ps 103:20–2. V. 3, "Hear, O kings! Give ear, O potentates! I will sing, will sing to YHWH, will hymn YHWH, the God of Israel," sounds liturgical as well; it is similar to Exodus 15:1, which many consider to be liturgical, and to various contexts, particularly in Psalms, which ask YHWH to listen. Yet, even though Judges 5 shares certain elements with various liturgies, it is difficult to characterize it in its entirety as a liturgy. The role of YHWH is not significant enough – note, for example, how sharply the opening of Judges 5 contrasts in this regard with Exodus 15, which opens in such a clear theocentric fashion: "I will sing to YHWH, for He has triumphed gloriously; horse and driver He has hurled into the sea." In addition, though Weiser and Gray attempt to explain why we have the muster of the tribes in vv. 14–18 in a liturgy, suggesting that they instead refer to "the procession of members of the sacred community present at the covenant 'sacrament' and the calling of the names of those who were not present" (Gray 1977: 19), this is not at all compelling, especially within a scholarly framework which no longer believes in an amphictyony that unified pre-monarchic Israel. Though the broad thesis that Judges 5 should be characterized as a liturgy is wrong, scholars must engage certain of the facts raised by Weiser and Gray about liturgical elements in the song.

In a recent study, Geoffrey P. Miller also critiques the various proposals for the Song's origin and function, and has suggested instead that it originated as a riposte, a verbal feud that restored Israel's honor by projecting the enemy's cultural stereotypes of Israel back on Israel's enemies (G.P. Miller 1998). In some ways, this idea builds upon various taunt motifs that earlier scholars had isolated within the song (Blenkinsopp 1961; Craigie 1969). This is a very suggestive theory, and Miller's reading can explain a great deal of this highly varied chapter, including the unexpectedly strong role that women have. Unfortunately, this theory is impossible to prove, since we really do not know what the "average Canaanite" felt about the "average Israelite" at the time of this poem's composition, and thus we cannot reconstruct what this poem might be responding to. Yet this article is valuable for its ability to think creatively, to realize that there are a wide variety of genres in ancient Israel which form critics have not yet isolated, and to suggest that any generic classification of Judges 5 must be sensitive to the diversity of material it incorporates.

Unfortunately, most guesses as to the origin and function of Judges 5 are just that – guesses. Part of the problem is endemic to form-criticism. We do not have the ancient life-settings; we can only reconstruct them, and buttress their plausibility by showing how they explain a collection of texts. Especially if we assume, with the majority of scholars, that (some early form of) this chapter is one of the earliest pieces of biblical literature, we cannot reconstruct the institutions of that period, thereby understanding how the poem might have fit in, and what its *Sitz im Leben* was. As noted earlier, this poem likely has a history, but unlike many Torah texts, because of this poem's poetic features, this history cannot be traced with much certainty, either in terms of the changes made over time, or when and by whom they might have been made. We can no longer recover the recontextualizations that the poem has gone through, namely the way sets of changes have responded to new periods and situations in which it was used. Thus, we cannot study in any historically responsible fashion various editions of the poem.

Despite these problems, I would like to suggest a new possibility for the genre of the Song. Given the problems involved, this will obviously be done in a very tentative fashion, and is merely an attempt to offer a context where the various elements of the poem can be explained. With the collapse of the model that biblical historical texts are historical in the sense of accurately depicting history, the question of why these texts that look like they are narrating history were written becomes very pressing. As noted earlier, this is not a matter of idle curiosity or merely a desire to have *Gattungen* that may pigeonhole each story. Rather, modern historians will consider the purpose of the story as crucial when they consider how to use a particular unit as history.

I would suggest that Judges 5 functioned as a poem recited before war, and one of its main functions was to muster the troops to battle. An earlier version might have had a different function, but this earlier version and its original function can no longer be reconstructed. The proposed purpose explains why the song was preserved – it was not a "victory song" of some ancient battle, that most likely would have been lost, but played a role in later Israelite life.

This possible function is supported by the existence of various types of pre-war rituals in various corpora of biblical literature. Deut 20:1–9 describes a complex ritual before going to battle (Rofé 1985); it includes a statement by the priest (vv. 3–4):

> Hear, O Israel! You are about to join battle with your enemy. Let not your courage falter. Do not be in fear, or in panic, or in dread of them. For it is YHWH your God who marches with you to do battle for you against your enemy, to bring you victory.

Psalm 20 should also be considered a prayer recited before war (Kraus 1988: 279). This explains such verses as: (v. 2),"May YHWH answer you in time of trouble, the name of Jacob's God keep you safe," (v. 6), "May we shout for joy in your victory, arrayed by standards in the name of our God. May YHWH fulfill your every wish," and vv. 7–10:

> Now I know that YHWH will give victory to His anointed, will answer him from His heavenly sanctuary with the mighty victories of His right arm. They call on chariots, they call on horses, but we call on the name of YHWH our God. They collapse and lie fallen, but we rally and gather strength. O YHWH, grant victory! May the King answer us when we call.

Psalm 20 is classified as a royal psalm, most likely recited by the king before battle (Gunkel and Begrich 1966: 140–71), but there are non-royal psalms of various sorts that were most likely recited before battle. Internal evidence suggests that Psalm 83, a lament of the community, was recited at the "imminent threat of a foreign invasion" (A.A. Anderson 1981: 2.595). God (v. 2) is asked not to be silent (v. 3), "For Your enemies rage, Your foes assert themselves." An alliance (v. 6) of various nations is listed (vv. 7–9). Most likely this alliance never attacked Israel, but reflects various re-uses that this psalm went through. The psalmist recalls past saving "events" (vv. 10–12), and asks YHWH to repeat them. Shame is a major theme of the psalm's conclusion (vv. 17–18).

These other biblical texts suggest what we otherwise would have guessed – that there were various types of prayers recited before battle. Many of the elements of Judges 5 fit elements seen in these texts. I would thus suggest the following understanding of the Song.

The Song has liturgical elements since it is meant to be used in a religious context: mustering people for an impending war, and in that context, calling on YHWH to help. The people are gathered together (v. 1), and are told to "bless YHWH" (vv. 2, 9), with the hope that YHWH will bless them. V. 3 is a fictionalized calling together of various foreigners, which parallels the similar fiction of addressing the nations found in the enthronement psalms, which emphasize YHWH's great power (Brettler 1989b: 145–56). The core of the Psalm is the recollection of YHWH's great saving actions in the past. For this reason, vv. 4–5 note the terror evoked even in the natural world when YHWH marched forth from Seir; most of the rest of the Song recalls YHWH's success against the Canaanites, in a battle which YHWH waged along with his heavenly host, the stars (v. 20) (Lindars 1995: 268–9). The shame of the enemy vanquished by a woman is recalled (vv. 24–7)[2] in order to recreate similar shame for the current enemies.

The core of the poem is clearly the recollection of the victory against the Canaanites. Though the lengths of the accounts are different, this is very similar to Ps 83:10–11: "Deal with them as You did with Midian, with Sisera, with Jabin, at the brook of Kishon – who were destroyed at En-dor, who became dung for the field." Psalm 106 recounts a long series of past events with the expectation of present salvation (v. 47; cf. v. 4): "Deliver us, O YHWH our God, and gather us from among the nations, to acclaim Your holy name, to glory in Your praise." Our poem has a similar structure – it notes God's past salvific acts, and concludes with a direct request (v. 31a): "So may all Your enemies perish, O YHWH! But may His friends be as the sun rising in might!" Some scholars, including the editor of BHS, do not believe that v. 31a is part of the song (Lindars 1995: 286). Their arguments are weak; without any question, v. 31 is poetry (note the parallelism between "your enemies" and "His friends"), and does not belong to the prose Dtr conclusion in v. 31b of "And the land was tranquil forty years." It might not belong to the "original" poem – whatever that might be – but is valuable evidence which should not be ignored that the event of battle is a likely setting for the poem. Indeed, exactly the same theoretical stance of viewing Israel's enemies as YHWH's enemies is seen in Ps 83:3, where it is *your* [=God's] enemies and foes that are highlighted.

The cursing and blessing, which is so central to the Song, reflects the difficulties of mustering. Though certain "holy war" traditions reflect the notion that all must "volunteer" to fight, it is unclear what period, if any, this might reflect. Usually, there is some choice in deciding whether or not to join a particular battle. Judg 12:1–6 reflects a notion that a group that was not included wanted to fight, while 8:1–17 concerns people who did not participate despite being asked. Again, it is irrelevant whether these particular episodes happened as described; these chapters reflect the idea that at times people had to be drafted into battle, and could not be compelled to serve.

Judges 5 is structured to convince groups of people to volunteer. It suggests that those who do might one day be memorialized in a similar poem, used to muster future generations, like the tribes mentioned in vv. 14–15a. Those who don't join in might suffer future embarrassment, like the tribes mentioned in vv. 15b–18. As is typical, the threat of embarrassment is more powerful than the promise of literary immortality, so this section is longer. The fate of those who refuse might be even worse than embarrassment – the city that does not join in might suffer the fate of Meroz, becoming paradigmatic for accursedness (v. 23).

In fact, even a single individual might be recalled for acts of valor. The poem indirectly stresses that no one is too insubstantial to be the hand through which YHWH offers national salvation. If vv. 24–7 can commemorate *forever* the actions of Jael, who is both a foreigner and a woman, and thus doubly marginal, any Israelite can certainly be chosen.[3]

Judg 5:28–30 mock the enemy by citing their assumption of victory. Quotations play a large part in this (v. 28b, 30). The enemy of course is wrong, and the quotations of the wise women are ironically twisted. Psalm 83 similarly contains two quotations of an enemy who wants to defeat Israel: (v. 5) "They say, 'Let us wipe them out as a nation; Israel's name will be mentioned no more'" and (v. 13) "who said, 'Let us take the meadows of God as our possession.'" Psalm 74:8 also attributes words to the enemy, in this case, to the enemy's heart. In any case, the evidence of these psalms suggests that Judg 5:28–30, which recount the enemy's activities and aspirations, would be very much at home in a psalm invoking God to help.

The first verse of the poem, v. 2, supports this reading. I will return to the difficult first half of the verse in a moment. The second half opens בהתנדב עם, "when the people (or armies) enlisted as volunteers."[4] The first two words of the verse, בפרע פרעות, are very abstruse, and no convincing interpretation has been given (Lindars 1995: 225–7). It had been fashionable to connect this to Num 6:5, and to interpret the verse as referring to loosening of hair, but this is unlikely, since hair is nowhere mentioned in Judges 5. The etymological evidence is not entirely clear or abundant (*HALOT* 3.970, s.v. פרע), but many words from this root connect to the sense of "being free or wild." I would thus suggest that the expression refers to all hell "breaking loose" (Lindars 1995: 226).

It is unlikely that v. 2 is really the beginning of the poem; more likely it is an incipit, noting when the poem would be recited. I would translate this incipit, which offers the context when the poem is used, colloquially as: "When all hell breaks loose, when the militia volunteer, bless YHWH." The fact that v. 3 has language typically associated with the opening of a poem (see Gen 4:23; Deut 32:1; Isa 1:2, 10; 32:9; Hos 5:1; Ps 49:2; 143:1; Job 33:1) favors reading v. 2 as an incipit of this type.

This understanding of the poem's genre has important implications for the use of the chapter by the modern historian. It is not an eyewitness account, and likely developed over time. Its main interest is not antiquarian, telling the events as they really happened. (This is even the case for the liturgical and victory poem suggestions.) Rather, it is trying to persuade and convince. It might very well use older traditions in doing so, but as generations pass, these traditions will naturally change to make the poem more effective at what it is trying to do. Contrasts will develop and will become more extreme, trying to convince the potential "inductee" to be like X and not to be like Y. Various traditions, concerning various battles, might become melded together. Though this process cannot be described in detail, the very existence of such a process suggests that the chapter cannot be used as a source for the early battles of the Israelites with the Canaanites.

There has been much discussion in the literature about the origin of Israel, and there is a growing consensus that the model that sees Israelite origins as from the native Canaanites is correct (Finkelstein and Na'aman 1994). As such, the various traditions and laws that deal with Israelite–Canaanite relations are extremely complex, since Israel is trying to differentiate itself from the group that it is closest to. This likely explains the law of the ban in Deut 20:15–18.[5] Thus, traditions of how the Israelites defeated the Canaanites were particularly important, and it is likely that several such traditions developed over time, and in some circles, influenced one another. Indeed, Ps 83:11, which situates the defeat of Sisera and Jabin at Ein-dor, is one such alternate tradition – that site is not connected to this battle in either Judges 4 or 5. Traditions, particularly traditions that are important for ethnic identity, change over time.

This understanding of change and development in poetic tradition differs sharply from the older models of professional poets carefully and precisely memorizing and reciting works exactly as they heard them. If such a model were correct, then even if the Song of Deborah were transmitted orally, it would be reliable and unchanging, not influenced by the new worlds in which the later reciters lived. Field work has shown that this model of static transmission is, however, incorrect. The various studies of Lord and Parry, as well as others, have incisively shown the faults of that model. As summarized by Ruth Finnegan, a leading scholar of oral literature: "[T]here is now much evidence leading us to doubt older assumptions that oral literature was naturally and inevitably formed through age-old transmission in unchanging forms over generations" (Finnegan 1977: 53). A similar point has been made by Niels Peter Lemche about biblical traditions (Lemche 1985: 379–83). Thus the fact that Judges 5 is poetry rather than prose has no bearing on how accurately it might have been transmitted or might reflect the true past.

Just because a position has been repeated for over a century, it need not be correct. This is the case for the various assumptions concerning the Song of Deborah. There is no reason to believe that it is an unchanged eyewitness account of the defeat of the Canaanites by some early tribal confederacy. Its date is uncertain, though much of it is likely among the earliest biblical literature, but it has undergone changes of all sorts over time. The standard genre attributions suggested of victory ode and liturgy are unlikely; instead it may be a poem recited at the eve of battle to muster the troops. This *Sitz im Leben* explains the features of the poem more satisfactorily than the suggested alternatives. It also has important implications for the use of the poem by the historian of antiquity. Such poems would naturally change over time, and cannot be used in a simplistic fashion to recreate the earliest history of Israel.

Doctrine by Misadventure?[6]

How should we understand the prose account of Judges 4? This question is more complex for Judges 4 than for other accounts in

Judges precisely because we have the "parallel" poetic account in Judges 5. Are these two totally separate accounts? Or has one somehow influenced the other (Younger 1991: 136–7 n. 1)? Ironically, the presence of the poetic version, another source, might make it more, rather than less, difficult to understand the development of chapter 4! Yet, partially under the influence of broader literary currents, the issues of textual influence and inner-biblical interpretation have gained scholarly attention (Fishbane 1985; Brettler 1995: 62–78; Sommer 1988), and have been applied to the Deborah–Barak material in Judges 4–5.

In *The First Historians: The Hebrew Bible and History*, Baruch Halpern, following Martin Noth, insists that the Deuteronomistic historian was a historian, and as such, was typified by "antiquarian interest" (Halpern 1988). A major piece of this argument builds on an earlier article by Halpern, revised for his book, suggesting that the author of Judges 4 was a historian who used Judges 5 as his source, and that the narrative in Judges 4 was created on the basis of a misunderstanding of that poetic source (Halpern 1983b).[7] This is an important argument for the modern historian of ancient Israel, since it suggests that ancient Israelite historians were characterized by antiquarian interest, and that other narrative passages might also be based on much more ancient texts.

Halpern's thesis is very strong: "Virtually no detail in Judges 4 is without an identifiable source; nearly all of them come from the poem, and from the historian's reconstruction of the event, based on a painstaking analysis of the poem" (Halpern 1988: 82). But is it correct?

It is very difficult to disprove Halpern's thesis. He does show how a later reader could misread the poem, and could creatively fill in the details, either from other biblical texts, from other traditions, or imaginatively. But is this likely?

Some of Halpern's suggestions, especially those concerning the death of Sisera by Jael, are reasonable because of close verbal associations between the prose and poetic accounts. Yet, others seem very far-fetched. How likely is it that a later reader of Judges 4 would think that only Zebulun and Naftali participated in the battle (4:6), based on a misreading of 5:14–17 that suggests that the other tribes waited at the gates (5:11), and only Zebulun and Naftali risked their lives (v. 18) (Halpern 1988: 80)? This is especially unlikely since Zebulun is mentioned along with Ephraim, Benjamin, and Machir in 5:14; thus if Zebulun fought, it is likely that these other tribes or groups did as well.

As intimated, the major problem with Halpern's thesis is that unlike other cases where we assume that one text interpreted another, such as Chronicles interpreting Samuel–Kings, there are very few direct verbal reverberations of the source in its supposed interpretation. It is such verbal allusions that are the key to determining literary interdependence.

In presenting his argument, Halpern is too quick to move from saying *if* one source influenced another, which would it be – and noting correctly that internal features suggest that it is the poetry that influenced the prose – to actually claiming that this is the case. He is aware of the fact that "[m]uch of the song has no reflex in the prose" (Halpern 1988: 95), and this seriously weakens his argument. Yet, his attempt to show why particular elements were ignored by the later historian are not very successful.

Halpern's model is too bookish. In addition, it confuses plausibility with probability. He does not concern himself with basic issues, such as: How likely is it that the Song of Deborah was widely known and authoritative in ancient Israel? May we assume that in the same way that the Chronicler knew earlier texts, the DtrH would have likely known the song? Finally, he does not do what historians must do – to examine his hypothesis of literary dependence against competing hypotheses, that the differences between the prose and poetry might be due to the fact that the author of the prose had access to other traditions not recorded in the poetry, rather than finding their origin in a close (mis)reading of the poetry. Certainly, the evidence of material preserved in the biblical canon suggests that all sorts of variants, even for the most crucial traditions (e.g. creation and Sinai), did exist.

More recently, Walter J. Houston has accepted Halpern's thesis that Judges 4 is based on chapter 5, but has suggested that the later source is not misunderstanding the earlier one, but interpreting it using methods similar to rabbinic midrash (Houston 1997). This is, in part, the result of rejecting Halpern's understanding of what the biblical historians were trying to do: "They were not researching ancient texts to make what they can of them for a reconstruction of the past. They are writing the story of their nation to confirm for them the faithfulness of their God..." (Houston 1997: 345). Houston's reminder that biblical history is theological is welcome, though not all biblical historical texts should be read as such – though we might suppose that all biblical historians were theists, this does not mean that all of their history focused on divine causality or theological lessons. Additionally, Houston's model is even more problematic than Halpern's because it really envisions "appli[cation of] quasi-midrashic methods to the text" (Houston 1997: 541). It is difficult to posit the existence in the biblical period of the Song of Deborah as a *text* which might be closely read and exposited in the same way that rabbis would later study the Bible.

Adjacent Competing Accounts

The basis for exploring Judges 4–5 in a separate chapter is that it is unique in Judges. It is neither a short story nor a cycle – it is the only case where two variants of the "same story" are preserved side by side. Why has this literary unit been created?[8]

Given the problem just noted of Houston's thesis, it is very hard to accept his proposal that the prose historian preserved the poetry so his source might be seen (Houston 1997: 546). The narrative order of the texts speaks against this proposal – it would be very odd to have the interpretation (Judges 4) before the text being interpreted (Judges 5).

K. Lawson Younger, Jr., building upon a literary study of Judges 4–5 by Athalya Brenner (Brenner 1990), suggests that the two accounts were preserved side-by-side because they were complimentary (Younger 1991: 109–46). He surveys Egyptian and Mesopotamian inscriptions, noting that prose and poetic accounts of the same event typically have some overlap, but have different emphases, much like Judges 4–5. The two accounts in Judges are unusual with respect to the ancient near eastern literature cited in that here different genres are cited side-by-side, but these accounts in Judges 4–5 should nevertheless be read as "simply complimentary ways of describing the great victory that took place" (Younger 1991: 134).

A different type of comparative approach is taken by Steven Weitzman, whose general work *Song and Story in Biblical Narrative* was cited earlier. Following James W. Watts, he compares the structure of Judges 4–5 to the Egyptian Piye Stele. Watts had suggested that the addition of the Song "enriches" the narrative (Watts 1992: 96); Weitzman modifies this idea, proposing that a final poem might be used at the end of a prose work to effect closure (Weitzman 1997: 35–6).

These proposals suffer from several weaknesses. The Piye Stele is too distant from Israel to function as a useful analogy; there is little evidence that the Egyptian historical tradition had a strong influence on ancient Israel. Furthermore, the suggestions of both

Younger and Weitzman, though they speak of the differences between Judges 4 and 5, underestimate the tension that is created by redacting the poem into its present place.

Nadav Na'aman, I believe, comes closest to recognizing why these two variants have been preserved:

> It seems to me that the Dtr historian used this historio-graphical device [=quoting several accounts of a single event] in order to present before his audience his divergent 'sources' on whose authenticity he did not wish to decide or was unable to do so... . In this respect the Dtr historian had an entirely different historical attitude toward his source material than the Chronicler, who always gave only one description of a given event. On the other hand, the authors of the Pentateuch used the same narrative technique as the Dtr historian and thus are much closer to him than to the Chronicler.
>
> (Na'aman 1994: 229)

What Na'aman is really pointing out, I believe, is that DtrH, like the redactor of the Torah, was not a historian in the etymological sense. This directly contradicts Baruch Halpern's central thesis. Etymologically, history refers to investigation, thus the collection and weighing of sources, determining which is right (Fornara 1983: 47). Thus, we are comfortable with certain aspects of the Chronicler, precisely because he used various historical and theological criteria to choose among the sources that he had. The contrast between the Chronicler and DtrH is quite clear concerning the events of 701, where the Chronicler reconciles the multiple sources now found in 2 Kings 18–20 (Childs 1967).

Thus, the doubling of accounts in Judges 4 and 5 causes competition between these two chapters, making us wonder such things as "How was Sisera killed?" "Where exactly was the battle?" "Was Jabin involved or not?" This is an essential feature of biblical narrative, which at least in its earlier forms, as evidenced in the Torah and the DtrH, is ahistorical in the sense that it combines accounts, rather than chooses between them. It is no different than the person who finishes Genesis 1–3 wondering how woman was created, or if animals were created before or after man. Though the "doubled account" in Judges 4–5 might be unusual in that one account is prose and one is poetry (but see Exodus 14–15), the doubling with variation should really not be surprising within biblical norms (Na'aman 1994: 228).

If anything, the real surprise is that there are not more such adjacent, competing accounts in Judges. Smaller adjacent competing accounts are found at the end of chapter 2 and the beginning of chapter 3, concerning the reasons why YHWH did not dispossess all of the Canaanites before Israel: as punishment (2:20–1), as a test (2:22; 3:4), or to teach them how to fight (3:2). It is likely that 8:1–3 and 12:1–6 reflect variant traditions about the Ephraimites. Perhaps the sources available for the Book of Judges were more limited than those used for Samuel or the Torah, which are full of variants. In any case, in evaluating the competing accounts in Judges 4 and 5, it is important to use predominant biblical norms of how history should be written, rather than importing contemporary scholarly ideas, where history is supposed to create a unitary picture based on investigation. Once we stop being anachronistic, we properly avoid seeing the juxtaposition in Judges 4–5 as a problem, and see it as well within the norm of one type of ancient Israelite "historical" writing.

6

WINDING DOWN
The Concubine of Gibeah

The stories of Judges end with Samson's death in chapter 16, and it is tempting to end the investigation of the Book of Judges with that, ignoring the final five chapters of the book, in which judges are absent. In fact, they may be seen as an independent, five-chapter unit, framed by "In those days there was no king in Israel; every man did as he pleased," which appears in 17:6 and 21:25, and in a shortened form in 18:1 and 19:1. Structurally and literarily this refrain joins together the two stories of the migration of the Danites in 17–18, and of the rape of the concubine and its aftermath in 19–21, and separates them from the preceding material.

For this reason, biblical scholarship has treated these five chapters as a totally separate section of Judges, disconnected from what appears earlier. Already in 1895, Moore introduced them with the title "Two Additional Stories of the Times of the Judges" (Moore 1895: 365). Soggin believes that they comprise "part three" of Judges, and like many scholars, considers them an "appendix" (Soggin 1981: 261). Following Crüsemann, he believes they are joined together because "they both deal with Levites residing in Ephraim who are not Ephraimites, who are wronged by the local population, and who somehow get involved with non-Israelite cities" (Soggin 1981: 263).

More recent scholars have viewed these five chapters as more integrated into the book. Yairah Amit, for example, correctly points to various ways that these chapters connect to the previous sections about judges (Amit 1999: 314–16). Robert H. O'Connell similarly feels that these units are thematically well-integrated into the book, and calls chapters 17–21 "Judges' Double Dénoument" (O'Connell 1996: 229). Various factors favor their positions. I agree, and suggest that both in terms of placement and meaning these five chapters reflect the fact that the narrative is winding down.

Judges 17–21 contrasts with other biblical books which conclude with true appendices. An appendix could be added to a biblical book if new material relevant to that book was found after the book had been formed. This is likely the case with 2 Samuel 21–4, which form a self-contained, organized miscellany (McCarter 1984: 16–19). The case for an appendix is even clearer for Jeremiah. Jer 51:64b reads: "Thus far the words of Jeremiah," and chapter 52 is "an appendix taken from the Deuteronomistic history" which serves to vindicate Jeremiah as a true prophet by showing that his prophecies of destruction transpired (Carroll 1986: 857–8).[1]

In contrast to Jeremiah 51, Judges does not clearly end at the conclusion of Judges 16. There is no major conclusion formula; rather some variation of the formula used at the end of each judge's term is found (O'Connell 1996: 49). More significantly, the beginning of Judges 17 is well integrated into the previous material; 17:1, "there was a man from … and his name was …" mimics Judg 13:2, the opening of the Samson story; this formula is found nowhere else in Judges. Furthermore, the amount of silver mentioned in 17:2, eleven hundred (shekels), is identical to the amount that each Philistine leader offered to Delilah in 16:5 (Zakovitch 1983: 169). Eleven hundred is not a stereotypical number, and its use in both chapters 16 and 17 indicates that chapters 17–21 are not merely an appendix, which is not connected to the previous material, but are integrated into the book. This will have important implications when we attempt to view the book of Judges in its entirety in Chapter Eight.

A Text of Terror

Women are central to the final episode in Judges in chapters 19–21. The unnamed concubine who is raped and butchered is first mentioned in 19:1. The actions done to her motivate everything that happens in the final two chapters. Women are explicitly mentioned in the last chapter as well, concerning the need to find wives for the remaining Benjaminite men. This focus on women is typical of Judges as a whole, which is exceptional in this respect within the Deuteronomistic History (O'Connor 1986: 277–93; Brenner 1993a; 1999; Bellis 1994: 112–39; Ackerman 1998). Certainly this is one of the features of the book that will need to be considered in the final chapter, when examining how the book as a whole coheres.

Without any question, Judges 19[2] is a "text of terror," and Phyllis Trible has done a great service in including this chapter in her study *Texts of Terror: Literary-Feminist Readings of Biblical Narratives* (Trible 1984: 64–91).[3] Trible highlights the way in which the rhetoric of the unit peripheralizes and dehumanizes the woman. In v. 18, when her master is looking for a place for them to stay overnight, he totally forgets about her, saying that he can find no one to offer *me* a place to stay overnight. In v. 25, when the man discards his concubine, the text does not even bother with the pronoun, reading literally "he expelled to them outside." The ambiguity at the end of the chapter, where it is unclear at what point the woman has died, evokes great horror. Using the methods of rhetorical criticism (Trible 1994), Trible comes to the following legitimate conclusion:

> Of all the characters in scripture, she is the least. Appearing at the beginning and close of a story that rapes her, she is alone in a world of men. Neither the other characters nor the narrator recognizes her humanity. She is property, object, tool, and literary device. Without name, speech, or power, she has no friends to aid her in life or mourn her in death. Passing her back and forth among themselves, the men of Israel have obliterated her totally.
> (Trible 1984: 80–1)

Though not all scholars have found Trible's reading compelling or sufficient (Jones-Warsaw 1993: 172–86; Kamuf 1993: 187–207; Bal 1993: 208–30; Müllner 1999: 126–42), she has been appreciated for bringing "the reader into solidarity with the female victims of the text in a manner in which few biblical scholars before her have had the sensitivity to do" (Jones-Warsaw 1993: 179). Ackerman, for example, builds upon Trible's reading, and notes a set of contrasts between this unnamed concubine and Delilah (Ackerman 1998: 239). Such readings are very important for contemporary readers, since they help to show the dangers of ancient authoritative texts for a contemporary society. Yet, Trible stated explicitly that among other things, this woman is a "literary device." This phrasing assumes, correctly I believe, that this story, like the other stories in Judges, is not here because it is reflecting the real ancient Israelite past. It is a created story. But within that broad frame of reference, it is crucial to ask: Why was this woman created as a rhetorical device? For what is she a literary device? To use J. Cheryl Exum's locution, why was this woman, in this situation, "raped by the pen" (Exum 1993: 170)?

Some Non-literary Readings of Judges 19

The subtitle of Trible's book is *Literary–Feminist Readings of Biblical Narratives*, which I take to mean readings of texts about and/or for women, using the tools of literary criticism. This goal is different from what I am suggesting in at least two ways: (1) Her reading begins with modern (theological) needs and concerns, rather than ancient norms;[4] (2) It is "literary" in a typical sense critiqued in Chapter Two, since it ignores the context that engendered the text.

Others have called for an approach that is broader than Trible's. Don Michael Hudson observes quite directly: "[T]his narrative is a product of a narrator who ingeniously portrays his message through the manipulation of his medium – not art for art's sake, but art for meaning's sake" (Hudson 1994: 53). Ken Stone is among those who employ anthropological approaches to cast light on the story, noting almost apologetically: "The limits to a strictly literary approach will then be transgressed so that the text can be placed in an anthropological frame" (K. Stone 1995: 89–90). His insights concerning the way in which homosexual rape imagery is used in the chapter in connection with a broadly Mediterranean code of honor and shame certainly highlight various aspects of the text that are otherwise easy to miss. Yet, this interpretation through such a general framework, without recourse to many of the specifics that shape this story, does not go far enough in explaining why this story was written, and why it took the particular shape that it has. Our world is full of implicit codes, social and other types – they do not all produce stories.

More compelling is Gale Yee's suggestion that Judges 17–21 should be read using the methods of ideological criticism, which "uses literary critical methods within a historical and social scientific frame in a comprehensive strategy for reading biblical texts" (Yee 1995: 146). She studies Judges 17–21 as a unit, and suggests that both stories there were written at the time of Josiah, the traditional date for the first edition of the Deuteronomistic history (McKenzie 1992: 163–4), and their goal was to consolidate Josiah's power and reform. That reform involved centralization of power, which is explicitly argued for in Judges 17–21. Furthermore, part of his reform involved the loss of power by the rural Levites; this explains, Yee suggests, why the Levites are so prominent, and depicted so negatively, in these five chapters.

The methodological approach of Yee is very commendable, particularly her attempt to find a logical context for the production of
the text. She certainly succeeds in offering such a *plausible* setting,
but her suggestion has several problems. She treats 17–21 as a single unit. Most scholars would disagree; the two stories are very different in tone and narrative underpinnings, and though they have
been edited together as a sub-unit in Judges, it is unlikely that they
were composed together. The dating of Judges is a very complex
issue; the final redaction might very well be post-Josiah, while
even the Josianic redaction likely incorporates a variety of earlier
sources (O'Connell 1996: 345–66). Thus, independent, specific evidence needs to be brought to bear on the Josianic date.

Yee's observation about the prominence of Levites in both stories is significant, but the interpretation of this data is quite complex, due to our uncertainty about the history of the Levites (Rehm
1992: 297–310). Indeed, it is unclear if she is correct in asserting
that the rural Levites were excluded from Jerusalem after Josiah's
reform; 2 Kgs 23:9 suggests that they were, but Deut 18:6–8 suggests that they may fully participate in the Temple ritual, on a par
with those who are native. It is unclear which view is historically
accurate, or for that matter, how accurate or idealized the depiction of Josiah's reform in 2 Kings 22–3 is.

An alternate reason may be given for why Levites figure so
prominently in these two stories. At some time, Levites were not
defined geographically or tribally, but incorporated individuals
who removed themselves from their families in divine service
(Albertz 1994: 58). They were landless, and are depicted as such in
Deuteronomy (e.g. 10:9; 14:27). For the narratives in chapters
17–18 and 19–21 to work, you need a landless person, who can
wander, and has no close kin. There is no indication in these chapters that the (rural) Levites are being condemned *as a class*, as necessary for Yee's reading.

Yee points out that ideological criticism may be used to tease out
what stands behind the text, based on a close reading of the text.
Her reading of this material is too schematic, as seen, for example,
in the way that she combines chapters 17–18 and 19–21 in her
analysis. More significantly, she does not pay sufficient attention to
the fact that Judges 19 in particular is a very learned text, full of
allusions to other biblical texts. This needs to be considered when
considering how, why and when it was written.

Judges 19 as a Learned Text

In the previous chapter, we looked at Halpern's model of Judges 4. He suggested that this text knew Judges 5, and was based on a close (mis)reading of that text. There were too few correspondences between these two texts to accept his model in that case, and alternative reasons could be posited for why there are certain similarities between these texts, and why the prose account of Judges 4 is shaped the way it now is. However, the model he presents for a text re-using various earlier texts that are now preserved in the Bible is reasonable, and will be helpful for understanding the shaping of Judges 19.

The clearest model for understanding this is the Book of Jonah, which has certain verses that are very similar to other sections that are preserved in the Bible. The most methodologically sensitive treatment of this material is by Jonathan Magonet, who notes: "When a phrase or sentence appears in two places in the Bible, it is possible that A quotes B, or that B quotes A, or that both have used independently a third source C" (Magonet 1976: 66). He develops various commonsensical criteria for deciding whether there is an allusion, such as how close the phrases are, how commonly they are used, and how much is shared between the texts (Magonet 1976: 65–84). He also develops a useful distinction between "quotations," which cite earlier texts, and "reminiscences," which verbally recall rather then closely mimic earlier texts. He finds seven texts that Jonah alludes to, but does not accept all of the suggestions for allusion raised by earlier scholars. This analysis does not highlight art for its own sake, to show that Jonah is an allusive book, but lays the groundwork, along with other formal features, for understanding the meaning of the book by seeing how a later text reuses an earlier text.

Though Magonet does not use the term, I would suggest that the evidence adduced by him characterizes Jonah as a "learned text." The very likely early post-exilic date typically posited for Jonah (Sasson 1990: 20–8), from a time period when a book culture became more predominant in Israel, makes it likely that the author of Jonah could have known and used a variety of earlier texts.

The case for Judges 19 (–21) is similar. Dating this pericope is difficult, and it is likely that it reflects "a long compositional history" (L.G. Stone 1988: 393). Certain features of the language of the chapter suggest that this history may have extended into the post-exilic period,[5] and thus its author/editor could have known earlier texts.

85

Judges 19 shares several phrases with the Sodom episode in Genesis 19; there is also a connection between the end of the chapter and 1 Sam 11:7. These connections are well-known, and are clearly offered in a chart in Burney's commentary (Burney 1970: 444–5), though as I will show later, his chart should be more comprehensive. The direction of borrowing is not immediately obvious, especially if the evidence for the late date of Judges 19 is not granted. In fact, at least in theory, it might be worth considering the option that they are both dependent on common motifs, of (spoiled) hospitality, and of mustering the people for war (Matthews 1992: 3–11; Soggin 1981: 289). Yet, by using the type of criteria suggested by Magonet and others, it is quite clear that Judges 19 has borrowed from other texts.

The case with Judg 19:29 (–20:1) borrowing from 1 Sam 11:7 is not certain, but is likely; 1 Sam 11:7 is a logical text, narrating the successful use of a symbolic action to muster the nation:

> He took a yoke of oxen and cut them into pieces, which he sent by messengers throughout the territory of Israel, with the warning, "Thus shall be done to the cattle of anyone who does not follow Saul and Samuel into battle!" Terror from YHWH fell upon the people, and they came out as one man.

In contrast, Judg 19:29; 20:1a narrate:

> When he [the Levite] came home, he picked up a knife, and took hold of his concubine and cut her up limb by limb into twelve parts. He sent them throughout the territory of Israel. Thereupon all the Israelites – from Dan to Beer-sheba and from the land of Gilead – marched forth.

The action of butchering the woman is highly unusual and unnatural, and certainly is not the typical way of mustering the army. In addition, the phrase about answering the call to arms in Judg 20:1 is longer than that in 1 Sam 11:7. Though I do not mean to claim that it is always the case that texts grow as they are transformed, it is more likely that "and they came out as one man" would be transformed in "thereupon all the Israelites – from Dan to Beer-sheba and from the land of Gilead – marched forth," than *vice versa*.

The evidence in the case of Genesis 19//Judges 19 is more conclusive. Susan Niditch is alone among recent scholars in claiming that Genesis has borrowed from Judges; she reaches this conclusion by claiming that the motifs that are common to both are crucial to the narrative in Judges, but are less deeply embedded in Genesis (Niditch 1982: 35–78). This evidence is not conclusive, since it might even be possible that the lack-of-hospitality motif was secondary to Genesis, but was later picked up by the author of Judges 19 as a key plot element as he constructed that chapter.

More recent studies which are interested in allusion, where direction of literary borrowing is important, rather than the broader issue of intertextuality (Penchansky 1992: 7–88), have correctly suggested that Judges has borrowed from Genesis.

Stuart Lasine has pointed out the most significant indicator for the "'one-sided' literary dependence" of Judges on Genesis (Lasine 1984: 38–9). Integral to Genesis 19 is Lot's offer to the crowd of his *two* daughters (v. 8). In contrast, the single concubine is the focus of Judges 19, except for v. 24, where the host says: "Look, here is my virgin daughter, and his concubine. Let me bring *them* out to you. Have your pleasure of *them*, do what you like with *them* [italics added]." The addition of this second woman is unnecessary for the narrative in Judges; as Lasine points out, "he [the old host in Judges] follows Lot's example so precisely that it is almost as though he were following a 'script'" (Lasine 1984: 39). This position has prevailed (Matthews 1992: 3–11), and may be supported by other evidence.

As I noted in reference to Judges 19 and 1 Samuel 11, it is proper to search for differences between two related texts, and to see if particular differences suggest the direction of borrowing. Thus, it is relevant that in Judg 19:24, the potential homosexual rape is called "that outrageous thing to this man," while in Gen 19:8, it is simply called "a thing." Both texts follow societal norms in viewing this act as an outrage; had the text of Genesis been copying Judges, it is unclear why it would have omitted this longer phrase.

Finally, though the core of correspondences between the two units is in Judg 19:20–24//Gen 19:2–8, there are several other cases where the two share phrases. For example, Judg 19:7 uses the relatively unusual root פצר, "to urge," which is found in Gen 19:3 and 9. The phrases "spend the night" and "leave early for your way" in Judg 19:9 are also found in Gen 19:2. Thus, the phrases that the two contexts share are close together, in a tightly knit context in Genesis 19, but are spread out in Judges 19. This is best explained by the author of Judges 19 utilizing Gen 19:2–8 as he composed the chapter, and distributing the references throughout, rather than the other way around.

Jeremiah Unterman has suggested that Judges 19 has also borrowed from the binding of Isaac in Genesis 22 (Unterman
1980:161–5). The use of the rare word for knife, מאכלת, in both
(Gen 22:6, 10; Judg 19:29) is very suggestive. Yet many of the other
similarities that Unterman finds between the two texts, such as
their use of the phrase "and X raised his eyes and saw," refer to
very common phrases, which might be shared accidentally, and
need not reflect borrowings. General thematic similarities, such as
noting "Both the cast of characters and the scene are similar..."
(Unterman 1980: 164) are not convincing. Finally, contrary to the
expectations that might be developed from post-biblical Judaism
and Christianity, that the binding of Isaac is a crucial, generative
text, it is never directly referred to in the Hebrew Bible. Unlike the
Sodom and Gomorrah motif, it is not very significant, and thus the
likelihood that Judges 19 refers to it is diminished.

Lasine has already criticized the position of several earlier scholars that the similarities between Judges 19 and other texts might be
seen as "'embellishments'" or "'irrelevant' and 'without much
coherence'" (Lasine 1984: 38). Though one could imagine cases
where a later author alluded to an earlier text to be fancy, or to
show off his knowledge, this is not typical (Sommer 1998: 6–31).
Thus, we must search for the way that these various allusions
cohere to form meaning.

Polemic and Allusion in Judges 19

Recent years have seen a revival of the position articulated in the
mid-nineteenth century that Judges 19–21 should be seen as an
anti-Saul polemic (Brettler 1989a: 412–13; Amit 1999: 341–50; 2000:
178–88). A variety of evidence connects this chapter to Saul. We
already saw that Judg 19:29 and 20:1 allude to Saul's battle against
Nahash the Ammonite in 1 Sam 11:7. The place names and tribal
affiliation in this final episode of Judges are closely connected to
Saul. Saul is from Gibeah (1 Sam 10:26), and is a Benjaminite (1 Sam
9:1). The city of Jabesh-gilead, so crucial to the continuation of the
narrative in Judges 20–1, has close affiliations with Saul: he rose to
fame when he liberated that city from Nahash (1 Sam 11:1), and the
residents of the city ultimately buried him and his family there (1
Sam 31:11–13). The city of Ramah, the birthplace and burial place
of Samuel (1 Sam 1:1; 28:3), and thus closely associated with Saul,
is mentioned in Judg 19:13. The city of Mizpah and the rock of
Rimmon, both mentioned in Judges 19–21, also play a role in the

Saul narratives (Amit 2000: 180–1). These multiple correspondences are too numerous to be coincidental.

These allusions also all function in the same way – they make Saul look bad. He comes from a tribe, indeed from a city of rapists and murderers, who are unwilling to own up to their wrongdoings. Through these allusions, chapter 19 in particular serves to de-legitimate Saul even before he becomes king. Though Yairah Amit deals with this chapter within the broader purview of "hidden polemic" (Amit 2000), the polemic here is hardly hidden at all.

This polemic also clarifies the reason why the Sodom pericope from Genesis 19 figures so strongly in this unit. Sodom is known for two things in the Bible: its great sin (e.g. Isa 1:10; 3:9; Ezek 16:46–9; Lam 4:6) and its crushing punishment by YHWH (e.g. Isa 13:19; Jer 49:18; Amos 4:11; Zeph 2:9). Both of these aspects are being alluded to here; the sins of the people of Gibeah, namely Saul, are heinous, and the house of Saul deserves the fate of Sodom; no future descendent of Saul possibly deserves to reign.

It is not clear when such a polemic would originate. Some feel that it would most likely develop early in the monarchical period, and be connected to the development of the ideology of the early Davidic monarchy (Jüngling 1981). This is certainly possible, though if I am correct, probable later language in the chapter suggests that this is unlikely. Much of the Book of Samuel, which is very difficult to date precisely, attempts to convince the reader that David is the legitimate successor of Saul (Brettler 1995: 91–111); such a polemic would only be needed if there were people who believed otherwise. As I have noted elsewhere (Brettler 1989a: 414–15), two of the latest biblical books provide us with evidence that the Saulide royal ideology did not die with David's or Solomon's accession to the throne. The fact that the post-exilic author of Esther chose a "new Saul," namely Mordecai from Benjamin, descended from Kish, to defeat Haman the Aggagite (contrast 1 Samuel 15) reflects the continued existence of a pro-Saul contingent in the post-exilic period. This is confirmed by the preservation of a lengthy genealogy of Saul and his family in 1 Chr 8:33–40. Much later rabbinic texts also seem to preserve traditions that laud Saul; this is quite surprising given the ultimate victory of David in the canon, and might suggest a continuing Saulide royal ideology.

The Question of Genre

Judges 19 is a learned, allusive, polemical text, arguing against the kingship of Saul, which is described early in the following Book of Samuel. The likelihood of this political reading is now widely recognized, and will be further supported in the next two chapters, which will show the same tendency in other parts of Judges as well. It is odd that the political reading of this story, dating from the nineteenth century, was ignored for much of the twentieth century, and did not again become popular until the end of the twentieth century. This is probably connected to the conservatism that predominated biblical scholarship in the post-Wellhausen period, both on the continent and in America (Thompson 1992: 1–84). Thus, scholars wanted to see historical texts as historical in as many ways as possible. Their *a priori* inclination was to see Judges 19 as reflecting a real battle, a real story of how the Benjaminites were almost decimated, but were allowed to recover, adding another piece of evidence to the obscure history of pre-monarchic Israel. This type of reading blinded scholars to the polemical nature of the text. Judges 19 does not reflect ancient events; rather, it creates them.

I suspect that this text was understood quite differently in antiquity. Its parallels to Jonah go well beyond their both being learned texts. I would argue that their learned nature makes them "studied," or fanciful, and the ancient reader appreciated them as such. Did the ancient readers of Jonah really believe that he was in the belly of a big fish for three days and three nights? Did they believe that the Ninevites repented, and that even their cattle participated in the repentance ceremony (3:7–8)? Similarly, did the ancient Israelites really believe that a woman would be cut up into twelve pieces and sent one to each tribe? In fact, it makes no sense to say that one piece would have been sent to Benjamin! Other details in the story are equally improbable. Would a man follow his concubine, especially after (v. 2) "she fornicated,"[6] and then have such a comfortable relationship with the concubine's father? This is an early marker that the story is not merely topsy-turvy (Lasine 1984: 37–59), but is not real. Even more indicative is the way that the typical 3–4 pattern is broken in vv. 3–8; instead of staying for three days and leaving on the fourth, the man stays for four days and leaves on the fifth! And what are the odds that the person the traveler should meet should just "happen to be" from the hill-country of Ephraim as well (v. 16, see v. 1)? I suspect that the ancient reader who read this text, and saw these features, and noted "didn't I hear this story already?" would not have classified it as history in the sense of a narrative that is depicting the (real) past.

Almost all of the comments that Uriel Simon offers for the learned Book of Jonah are appropriate for Judges 19: "The book of Jonah lacks the traditional hallmarks of historical writing... We may ask about its historical likelihood... The repentance of the Ninevites ... is less plausible than the physical possibility of the miracles that happened to Jonah" (Simon 1999: xviii–xvi). The ultimate result is that internal markers within Jonah suggest that it be treated as a story rather than as history.

It would be incorrect, however, to call works such as Jonah or Judges 19 historical fiction. The author of Jonah, at least, who refers to "the king of Nineveh" (3:6) and depicts Nineveh as much larger than it was (3:3) does not share the goal of writers of historical fiction of getting the background picture right. The goal is to teach. Jonah is much more ambiguous in terms of its lesson than Judges 19, perhaps because Jonah is so theological, whereas Judges 19 is more political. But they both use the garb of history to teach.

J. Cheryl Exum is right that the concubine is "raped by the pen." She has as much reality as the fish which swallowed and then vomited up Jonah. She was "borrowed" and "fleshed out" from Genesis 19, and reworked a bit. Certainly, what was done to her in Judges 19 was not impossible in ancient Israel, just as it is not impossible today. However, if like Trible, we make that our sole focus, we misread the text from a historical–literary perspective, missing many significant clues. A woman is dismembered in a text to express the collapse of pre-monarchical society (Niditch 1982; Lasine 1984), and more significantly, the inability of Saul to correct that collapse. When read fully, following its genre clues, the text really says: "In those days there was no king in Israel (17:6; 18:1; 19:1; 21:25) and Saul wouldn't be much better, either."

7

A CONCLUSION THAT
BECAME AN INTRODUCTION

Judges 1:1–2:10 comprises the introduction to the Book of Judges.[1] It is followed by a paradigmatic account, which recounts the pattern that each major judge, to a greater or lesser extent, follows (O'Connell 1996: 19–57). In the later nineteenth century, and for much of the twentieth century, this section of chapters 1–2 was seen as an early tradition concerning the conquest of Israel, which differed from Joshua in several respects. This is reflected, for example, in the works of the great German and British scholars, Julius Wellhausen and S.R. Driver.

In the *Prolegomena*, Wellhausen notes that Judges is "parallel" to Joshua. Unlike the Book of Joshua, however, Joshua does not lead all Israel in Judges; "[t]he incompleteness of the conquest is acknowledged unreservedly" (Wellhausen 1973: 358). Wellhausen feels that chapter 1 is "incomparably more historical than that in the Book of Joshua, where the whole thing is done at once with systematic thoroughness" (Wellhausen 1973: 359). Driver, who by adopting Wellhausen's schema for understanding the development of the Bible was responsible for the influence of Wellhausen on the English speaking world, paraphrases Wellhausen. He opens his discussion of Judges 1:1–2:5 by noting: "This section of the book consists of fragments of an old account of the conquest of Canaan – not by united Israel under the leadership of Joshua, but – by the individual efforts of the separate tribes" (Driver 1972: 162). He states that this material comes from "excerpts from what was once a detailed survey of the conquest of Canaan" (Driver 1972: 163). Many more recent works accept these old conclusions. For example, the biblical history of J. Alberto Soggin notes: "In Judg. 1.1–2.5 we have a more fragmentary account of the conquest; it is now recognized to be closer to the events... " (Soggin 1984: 141–2).

This position made sense within the framework of older biblical scholarship, where the natural question when there were two contradictory texts about the same event was: "Which of the competing accounts is more accurate?" It was obvious that Judges 1 should be chosen over Joshua, since Judges 1 is shorter and less ideologically developed than the Book of Joshua. We now recognize, however, that these scholars were really framing the question incorrectly, by assuming that at least one of the preserved traditions should be (relatively) accurate. The correct initial question, we now appreciate, is: "Is either of these traditions to be considered an accurate reflection of the conquest of Israel?"

The problems of Judges 1 were already highlighted in the middle of the last century, when G. Ernest Wright noted that the chapter

> [P]resents many problems, because it is a collection of miscellaneous fragments of varying dates and varying reliability. To represent it or even some part of it as the earliest and most reliable account of the conquest of Canaan is to oversimplify the whole problem.
>
> (Wright 1946: 109)

Slowly, this position has influenced other scholars. By 1975, A.G. Auld could argue for a "reconsideration" of the older view, noting contradictions of content and style within the introduction that clearly suggest that it is a composite work that dates from a late period (Auld 1975: 261–85). A decade later, E. Theodore Mullen, Jr., echoing (his teacher) Wright, could speak of this material "as a collection of miscellaneous fragments of varying dates and varying reliability" (Mullen 1984: 33–64).

This new perspective raised a whole new set of questions, which I will attempt to explore in this chapter: If Judg 1:1–2:10 are not an accurate description of the conquest of the land, what are they? How do they connect both to Joshua, which they seem to parallel from a chronological perspective, and to Judges, to which they are now connected? Finally, following Wright, Auld, Mullen, and others, once these chapters are not seen as an accurate reflection of the historical conquest, we must subject them first to an internal analysis, at which point all sorts of issues and problems arise: Why is such a variety of material incorporated? How is it organized? Why, for example, does it twice narrate the death of Joshua (1:1 and 2:8)?

The rest of the chapter will attempt to answer many of these questions by first examining the place of this material within, or more precisely, between, the Joshua–Judges complex. After establishing that (an earlier form of) this section originally belonged to Joshua, I will highlight clues that suggest it has been intentionally moved to serve as the introduction to Judges. Finally, I will explore the structure and meaning of the unit in its current home, as the introduction to Judges.

It may seem odd that I am dealing with the introduction of Judges at the end of this book, immediately before the Conclusion. This was done for several reasons. It allowed the core of the Book of Judges, chapters 3–16, concerning the major judges, to stand together at the beginning of this book. More significantly, the beginnings of books are extremely important in terms of highlighting a book's main themes and interests. This, I believe, is the case with Judges as well. Thus, the argument concerning the purpose of this introduction will bring us directly to the "Conclusions," where I will suggest that the ideology seen in the structure of the introduction is operative in the book as a whole.

The Original Conclusion of Joshua[2]

The previous chapter, in denying the likelihood that Judges 17–21 should be considered an appendix to Judges, briefly examined various biblical books that have appendices, and discussed what these appendices look like. It is striking that Judg 1:1–2:10 has been typified in almost exactly the same terms used of the appendix to Samuel, in 2 Samuel 21–4: "a conglomeration of material … miscellany, a repository of diverse material" (McCarter 1984: 16). This structure is not typical of the beginning of biblical books, which though they are not always unified, are typically more tightly constructed.

The very close correspondences between the original end of Joshua[3] and the end of this introduction to Judges are well-known, and are illustrated below:

> Josh 24:28–31: (28) Joshua then dismissed the people to their allotted portions. (29) After these events, Joshua son of Nun, the servant of YHWH, died at the age of one hundred and ten years. (30) They buried him on his own property, at Timnath-serah in the hill country of Ephraim, north of Mount Gaash. (31) Israel served YHWH during

the lifetime of Joshua and the lifetime of the elders who lived on after Joshua, and who had experienced all the deeds that YHWH had wrought for Israel.

Judges 2:6–9: (6) When Joshua dismissed the people, the Israelites went to their allotted territories and took possession of the land. (7) The people served YHWH during the lifetime of Joshua and the lifetime of the older people who lived on after Joshua and who had witnessed all the marvelous deeds that YHWH had wrought for Israel. (8) Joshua son of Nun, the servant of YHWH, died at the age of one hundred and ten years, (9) and was buried on his own property, at Timnath-heres in the hill country of Ephraim, north of Mount Gaash.

These correspondences present yet another problem, and a clue; as Eamonn O'Doherty notes: "It is extremely unlikely that in two succeeding books the conclusion of one would be identical to the introduction of the next" (O'Doherty 1956: 3–4).

The beginning of the answer lies in the observation of Rudolf Smend that Judg 2:6–9 should be considered a *Wiederaufnahme* or resumptive repetition of Josh 24:28–31 (Smend 1971: 506). The literature on this device suggests that it has various purposes (Brettler 1997: 604 n. 13). It may be used by a single author, especially to indicate the simultaneity of two events (Talmon 1978: 9–26). This use would not fit the material in Judges 1 and the beginning of Judges 2. Its more typical use is by an editor, who through this device marks the return to the original text which he has supplemented. This may be seen very clearly in many biblical texts, but most especially in books like Deuteronomy, which were subjected to heavy editing (Levinson 1997: index s.v. editorial devices: repetitive resumption [*Wiederaufnahme*]). Priestly editors often use this device when adding to an earlier document; this explains why the summary coda of Lev 26:46, "these are the laws, rules, and instructions that YHWH established, through Moses on Mount Sinai, between Himself and the Israelite people" is repeated in 27:34, after the secondary insertion of the laws in chapter 27: "These are the commandments that YHWH gave Moses for the Israelite people on Mount Sinai." The variation between the original statement and its reformulation is typical of the *Wiederaufnahme*.

It is even possible that our modern perspective, which makes a clear distinction between the books of Joshua and Judges, is incorrect. This distinction is based on all biblical manuscripts, and also on the fact that modern historians of the biblical period have distinguished between the period of the conquest, as seen in Joshua, and the period of transition to monarchy, as seen in Judges. This, however, is a scholarly construct, which recent historical study of the Bible has denied. In fact, Judg 21:24, "Thereupon the Israelites dispersed, each to his own tribe and clan; everyone departed for his own territory," uses the words "tribe" and "territory" that typify Joshua, thereby connecting Judges to Joshua.

Joshua–Judges might have even been copied together on a single scroll, and might have been viewed as a single work, much like Samuel, Kings, Chronicles, or Ezra–Nehemiah, until these works were divided into two parts by the LXX (Zakovitch 1983: 177). Joshua–Judges would be the same size as many of these works, and as the Major Prophets; separately they are short for biblical books. Unfortunately, very few copies of Joshua and Judges have been preserved from the Dead Sea, where, for example, adjacent books such as Genesis–Exodus and Leviticus–Numbers are sometimes copied together (DJD 9, 18), so there is no outside evidence to confirm the conjecture that Joshua–Judges might have been viewed as more of a single unit than their current canonical shaping suggests. In any case, the isolation of the *Wiederaufnahme* suggests that at some point in its history, Judg 1:1–2:10 belonged more to what preceded than to what followed.

A New Introduction to Judges

It is not clear when (an early form of) these verses broke away and became associated instead with Judges. Perhaps the contradictions between this appendix and the main theme of Joshua, of a complete conquest of the land of Israel in which all of the people of Israel participated, facilitated this move. Perhaps some general desire for symmetry prevailed: the movement of this material flanks the stories about the judges with an introduction and a conclusion in which judges are absent.

Once this material was shifted from an appendix to an introduction, several changes were made. The most obvious was that a proper opening for Judges needed to be created; this was done through the addition of the words: "After the death of Joshua," which was most likely modeled on the introduction of Joshua

(1:1): "After the death of Moses." The person responsible for this change must not have realized that this addition contradicted the end of the appendix, specifically 2:8, which (again) narrates Joshua's death.

Judges 2:10 was also created *after* this section was moved into its current place, introducing Judges. It reflects a narrow interpretation of Josh 24:31//Judg 2:7, which notes: "The people served YHWH during the lifetime of Joshua and the lifetime of the elders who lived on after Joshua and who had witnessed all the marvelous deeds that YHWH had wrought for Israel." By this I mean that in typical (proto-)rabbinic style, this verse is interpreted to suggest that the people served YHWH *only* during the time of Joshua. This verse, whose close verbal similarities to Josh 24:31//Judg 2:7 suggest that it was created on the basis of interpretation, serves as a brilliant topical segue to the following verse (Judg 2:11), "And the Israelites did what was offensive to YHWH ...," though the terminology for disobedience used in the two adjacent verses is different.

This model for the change in status of some form of Judg 1:1–2:10 from an appendix that was tied to what preceded, to an introduction that is connected to what follows, cannot be proven. It is doubtful that some manuscript will be found in which Joshua ends with these verses, and Judges begins with 2:11. Yet, the proposal suggested cannot be dismissed as pure conjecture because it helps to explain many of the very strange features of Judg 1:1–2:10. Its ultimate merit would need to be judged against other proposals which attempt to explain the odd features of the current introduction to Judges.

A Judah-centric Introduction

No criteria are available to determine with certainty which parts now in Judg 1:1–2:10 were part of the earlier appendix to Joshua, and which have been added, deleted, or revised as a result of the new place of this pericope at the head of the book. Some changes were suggested above. In addition, it is likely that at some point, 1:1–2:

> After the death of Joshua, the Israelites inquired of YHWH, "Which of us shall be the first to go up against the Canaanites and attack them?" YHWH replied, "Let the tribe of Judah go up. I now deliver the land into their hands,"

the introduction of the book and 20:18, "They proceeded to Bethel and inquired of God; the Israelites asked, 'Who of us shall advance first to fight the Benjaminites?' And YHWH replied, 'Judah first,'" from the last episode in Judges were formed to parallel each other. In addition, both 2:6 and 21:24 use similar language to describe the people returning to their ancestral homes. These correspondences are too strong to be coincidental; they create an inclusion and frame the book. More significantly, they suggest that 1:1–2:10 should not be seen as an appendix which "happened" to migrate, but was at some point integrated into the book through changes at the book's beginning and/or end. Thus, as noted above, understanding this section's structure and meaning may offer an important interpretive key for understanding the book as a whole.

In 1967, Moshe Weinfeld spoke of the "patent Judean tendentiousness" of this unit (Weinfeld 1967: 94–5 n. 1). He has supported this contention in a more recent article which concludes:

> There is no doubt that the document of Judges 1 tendentiously serves to glorify the tribe of Judah and to lessen the stature of "Israel" in the north. This tendency, which is interlocked with a criticism of Benjamin, derives, it seems, from circles from the house of David who sought to show that Judah, David's tribe was that which stood behind the conquest of the land and not the tribes of the North.
>
> (Weinfeld 1993: 398)

Weinfeld is not alone in singling out the significance of Judah in this opening section. The diagram on the following page, from a recent article by K. Lawson Younger, Jr. is very instructive.

The evidence concerning the prominence of Judah in this unit is not open to dispute; the interpretation of this evidence, however, is varied. What is the role of Judah in this unit, and how does it compare to the role(s) of the other tribes (Brettler 1989a: 399–402)?

The material about Judah incorporates several episodes of various types; some of it is paralleled in Joshua, and might have been copied from Joshua after the appendix became an introduction, while other material has no parallel in Joshua. The language is not strongly Dtr, so it is unlikely that a Dtr editor of Judges composed this new material. More likely, it is material that was part of the appendix to Joshua, or additional material that an editor inserted once the pericope moved to introduce Judges.

The bars represent the length of textual verbiage for each tribe.

Figure 7.1 The number of verses describing each tribe in Judges 1.

Reproduced with permission from Younger (1994: 218) Copyright Eisenbraums Inc., Indiana.

Judah is not only significant in terms of the number of verses that it occupies, but also in terms of the actions attributed to it. The answer to the oracle in 1:1 asking who should first fight the Canaanites is an unambiguous (v. 2) "Judah shall go up. I now deliver the land into their hands." The humiliation of Adoni-bezeq (v. 6) illustrates the total power of Judah, and the tradition that he was brought to Jerusalem (v. 7), thus asserting that Jerusalem is under Judean control, establishes the Judean right over the later national capital. This assertion is repeated in v. 8, and extended in the following verse to Judah's conquest of everything – of "the Canaanites who inhabited the hill country, the Negeb, and the Shephelah." To our ears it might be jarring that Adoni-bezeq is delivered to Jerusalem (v. 7) before the city is captured by Judah (v. 8), but this should be seen as a doubling of traditions which highlights Judah's role in conquering and controlling the city. They were likely read in a non-chronological fashion, and seen as mutually reinforcing rather than contradictory.

Judg 1:10–15, 20 parallel Josh 15:13–19, and are most likely borrowed from Joshua. In Joshua, these verses fit their context, and follow the introduction of Caleb in 5:13, while in this context, Caleb is introduced quite abruptly. The abrupt introduction of Caleb in Judg 1:12 suggests that an editor has copied over these verses (with slight variants) from Joshua. They concern the role of Caleb, whom later tradition viewed as an important Judean tribal leader (see above, p. 26) of Hebron. Hebron was a crucial Judean city, closely tied according to tradition to the Davidic monarchy; it was from Hebron that David first served as King (2 Sam 2:11). The importance of this city as well is sanctioned here.

The following verses (16–19), which disrupt the connection between vv. 15 and 20, and thus were likely added to this introduction subsequent to them, add to Judah's conquests, even narrating that Judah conquered the Philistine cities (v. 18). This would stand in remarkable contrast to Saul, who could not defeat the Philistines, and died in battle against them. V. 19 summarizes Judah's accomplishments: "YHWH was with Judah." Following the Book of Joshua, this resonates with Josh 6:27, which states: "YHWH was with Joshua"! The ideal leadership of Joshua is transferred, after his death, to the entire tribe of Judah. The continuation of the verse explains why Judah's conquest was not absolute – it was "impossible" (כי לא) to dispossess the valley dwellers due to their superior technology (Weinfeld 1993: 396). The verse, however, makes quite clear that this partial failure is no fault of Judah's.

Judg 1:21, "The Benjaminites did not dispossess the Jebusite inhabitants of Jerusalem; so the Jebusites have dwelt with the Benjaminites in Jerusalem to this day," is a remarkable revision of Josh 15:63, "But the Judites could not dispossess the Jebusites, the inhabitants of Jerusalem; so the Judites dwell with the Jebusites in Jerusalem to this day." The general consensus of scholarship is that failure to conquer Jerusalem is transferred from Judah to the neighboring Benjamin (Mullen 1984: 46; Weinfeld 1993: 396); clearly, this is done to glorify Judah, and, matching the final episode of Judges, to deprecate Benjamin.

It is difficult to know how to read 1:22–6, which seem to narrate the successes of the house of Joseph. It is significant that these successes are immediately tempered by the failures of both Manasseh and Ephraim in vv. 27–9. In addition, it is noteworthy that in contrast to Judah, which practiced a complete ban on the native Canaanites in v. 17, the House of Joseph lets someone escape (vv. 25–6); this may reflect a negative value judgment (cf. 1 Samuel 15). Weinfeld suggests that the use of deceit rather than warfare to capture the city is also meant to reflect negatively on Joseph (Weinfeld 1993: 397). In any case, the conquest of the House of Joseph is much less complete than that of Judah. This whole episode serves in various ways as a transition from the great accomplishments of Judah to the failures of the following tribes.

The rest of the chapter, concerning various northern tribes, contains various material that has as its theme that tribes "did not dispossess" various peoples. Some of the material has parallels in Joshua, and may be copied from there; other material has no parallels, and may be original to the appendix of Joshua. The key point, however, is the failure of these non-Judeans to fully conquer their tribal allotments. This is emphasized through the strange narrative in 2:1–5, which takes place at Bochim, near Gilgal in Northern Israel, that emphasizes the failure of the *northern tribes* to complete the conquest.

YHWH is present, indeed is mentioned twelve times in this introduction. This fact does not make the unit into a predominantly theological rather than political unit. Politics and theology cannot be totally separated in the ancient world (see below, pp. 114–15). Yet, there are certain passages which are more interested in human causality (read: politics) and others that care more about divine causality (read: theology). The two are often intertwined in different ways, to different extents (Seeligmann 1963: 385–411; Amit 1987: 385–400). Here, in the introduction, the emphasis is on the tribes and their fortunes – a political interest. As elsewhere, this is sanctioned by God – a theological perspective – but this perspective does not dominate. Instead, the main interest throughout the introduction is in expressing the relative power of Judah.

The fact that the emphasis is on centers of power comes through clearly from the ordering of the traditions. The editor/author has used "popular folkloristic traditions and historical lists" (Weinfeld 1993: 392), but as Younger shows in a graphic chart, organizes them geographically, from South to North. Dan is depicted anachronistically last, in its northern position, where it will ultimately reside, though according to Judges 17–18, this has not yet happened. This emphasis on geography, and on the good tribes versus the bad tribes, with Judah winning, suggests that the material is not ordered to show any "moral or spiritual decline," as suggested by Younger (Younger 1994: 217). The following comments by Mullen are more on the mark:

> The intent is to protect and project the significance of Judean primacy and to explain why Judah emerged in the monarchical times as the dominant tribe. Only Judah has been selected as a leader by Yahweh (1:2); only this tribe has instituted the *ḥerem* (1:17); only the Judeans have acted in accord with the pronouncement of Moses (1:20). The other tribes, despite minor successes (1:22–6), had acted against the laws of Moses (Deut 20:11) in leaving the Canaanite and Amorite in the land and subjecting them to the *corvée* (1:27–35).
>
> (Mullen 1984: 53)

Mullen's comments, which assume that the author was interested in the issues of his own day, are an important corrective to the earlier opinions concerning Judges 1, which saw it as an old, accurate tradition about the conquest that was precisely preserved in Judges even though it differed from the predominant account in Joshua. Mullen indirectly highlights the main issue that the conclusion will highlight: Given that authors are typically interested in "organizing the past in accordance with the needs of the present" (Febvre 1973: 41), what background may we propose that will make the Book of Judges in its entirety fall into place?

8

CONCLUSION: THE CENTER DOES COHERE

A paradigm shift, or more correctly several paradigm shifts, have occurred over the last few decades in biblical studies. These have been highlighted indirectly in the first two chapters of this book. One shift has been in the area of the Bible and history, and much of biblical scholarship has moved away from a simplistic model of the Bible as history, and has begun to treat the Bible as a more "normal" ancient text, rather than a privileged one. It is no longer taken at face value, and much more attention has been given to the period that various sources derive from, and the extent to which ideology rather than actual historical events have shaped the biblical narrative (Brettler 1995: 1–7).

A second paradigm shift has occurred in the area of the literary study of the Bible. At the end of the nineteenth century, models from Pentateuchal scholarship still dominated the study of much of the Bible, including Judges. Moore, for example, could speak of J and E in Judges (Moore 1895). Noth's 1943 study, which "created" the Deuteronomic history (Noth 1981), has been extremely influential (McKenzie and Graham 1994), and quickly led to the demise of the older source-critical theories. Within several decades, however, these were replaced by new source-critical theories, which suggested models for how Judges developed from its pre-deuteronomistic core to its current deuteronomistic shape (Richter 1963; 1964), and now a wide variety of theories have been developed concerning the number of stages of editing the book has gone through (O'Connell 1996: 347–66). Like the earlier source-critical theories, these theories concerning layers of redaction have emphasized the lack of consistency in the book.

Modern literary study, however, has downplayed, or often even disregarded these types of observations, highlighting instead the book's coherence. This is true even of studies which from their titles might appear otherwise. For example, J. Cheryl Exum's "The Centre Cannot Hold: Thematic and Textual Instabilities in Judges," despite its title, really argues that the instabilities, particularly as they relate to the theological problems raised by the book, help to unify it (Exum 1990). Similar positions have become extremely popular recently. Guest, in an article called "Can Judges Survive without Sources?" answers an emphatic "yes," arguing that "the narratives in Judges cohere so well, because they derive solely from the hand of one writer who produced a well-crafted work" (Guest 1998: 60). The most recent commentary on Judges begins from a similar perspective, noting: "The present examination is interested in how the entire book of Judges functions as a unified literary document…. Judges is a well-integrated theological narrative which builds its story and supports its thesis until its conclusion" (Schneider 2000: xiii).

These notions of a "well-crafted work" or a "book," which now predominate the field, seem to fly in the face of the evidence developed in chapter four, which showed that the story of Samson does not cohere, despite various attempts to force it into literary straitjackets. The insistence that the book is a unity also does not sit well with the cumulative evidence developed throughout this book, which highlighted the extent to which differences of all sorts are found within Judges. The cycle is fundamentally different than the short story, and both are different from Judges 4–5, which included parallel prose and poetic accounts. Chapter three even highlighted how different three different short stories were from each other, and certainly a longer study would show how the various longer cycles have little in common. Chapters six and seven emphasized how different the introduction and conclusion of the book, where judges are absent, were from the middle of the book, and at various places the tension between the accounts of the major judges and the minor judges was noted. It would thus seem that I fundamentally disagree with those who argue for the book's coherence.

As I will show later in this chapter, I do not believe that there is *very* strong coherence in the book. Yet, I also do *not* believe that the book is a result of a haphazard collection of texts, or a random set of additions to an original core. Its final shape seems to reflect shaping toward particular goals that I would broadly identify as political. These goals are reflected in most parts of the book, and offer it a broad type of coherence. Much of the material, from most of the diverse parts of the book, fits this model. This will be argued later in the chapter, once a broader framework for looking at coherence is presented.

It is impossible in this context to present and evaluate all of the various proposals for coherence and structure proposed for Judges. Instead, I have chosen to examine two very different proposals, which raise more general issues. I will first explore Gooding's proposal of a formalistic structure for the book (Gooding 1982). This is followed by an exploration of the work of Mieke Bal, a leading narratologist who is particularly interested in feminist issues. Bal has taken a special interest in Judges, and has written a trio of books on Judges, including *Death & Dissymmetry: The Politics of Coherence in the Book of Judges* (Bal 1988a; cf. Bal 1987; 1988b). The examination of the works of Gooding and Bal is meant to highlight certain issues which need to be considered in terms of examining the book's coherence. These issues will offer the background for my proposal that the book does cohere, but on the editorial rather than compositional level, and that it should be connected to political issues in ancient Israel.

A Symmetric Schema for Judges

Based on "notable features" that certain texts in Judges have in common, particularly similarities and contrast, Gooding has proposed the following structure for Judges:

A. Introduction Pt. 1 (1:1–2:5)
  B. Introduction Pt II (2:6–3:6)
    C. Othniel (3:7–11)
      D. Ehud (plus Shamgar) (3:12–31)
        E. Deborah, Barak, Jael (4:1–5:31)
          F. Gideon (6:1–8:32)
        E'. Abimelech (plus Tola, Jair) (8:33–10:5)
      D'. Jephthah (plus Ibzan, Elon, Abdon) (10:6–12:15)
    C'. Samson (13:1–16:31)
  B'. Epilogue I (17:1–18:31)
A'. Epilogue II (19:1–25)

(Gooding 1982: 77*–78*)

The implications of this chart are clear to Gooding; they suggest that "there is every evidence to suggest that each piece of source material has been selected and arranged with a careful eye to its contribution to the effect of the whole," and thus the Book of Judges most likely is "the work of one mind" (Gooding 1982: 77*).

The analysis of Gooding, which others have followed (Globe 1990), is open to the various critiques noted in Chapter Two, concerning Fokkelman's analysis of the tower of Babel story. It is odd, for example, that the center of Judges according to Gooding's model is the Gideon material, which is really quite far from the actual center of the book. His C and C' do not work as parallels: C, the Othniel story, is four verses long, while C', about Samson, is four chapters long! The basis for creating the C–C' parallel, namely contrasting attitudes concerning wives and foreigners (Gooding 1982: 73*), is too broad, and ignores the many ways in which these two units are fundamentally dissimilar. In general, Gooding's parallels are created through themes, rather than verbal similarities – this is particularly subjective. There is also a certain arbitrariness in the entire structure: Why does Othniel count as his own unit, but Shamgar does not? Is it certain that Abimelech deserves his own unit, or is it more suitable to consider him as part of a broader Gideon–Abimelech pericope? How do the three minor judges appended to Jephthah parallel Shamgar, whose narrative is not structured like the minor judges, and who is attached to Ehud?

In sum, the model offered by Gooding is not satisfactory. It is coherence imposed. As the previous chapters have shown, Judges has been compiled from a very broad range of sources, as broad or perhaps even broader than that found in any other biblical book. As such, it would have been impossible for any editor to bring this material together into a symmetrical structure, and only by using the vaguest thematic criteria and by ignoring counter-evidence, especially concerning the lack of size balance between the various units, can a symmetrical structure be imagined. Bal is certainly correct when she notes the fallacy of "chiastic structures, ring compositions, and the like" (Bal 1988a: 32), and proposes a different type of coherence for the book.

Women as the Center of Judges

The role of women in Judges is rich and varied, particularly when compared to other biblical works incorporated into the DtrH. Several studies of these women have been written (O'Connor 1986; Exum 1993: 61–93; 170–201; 1995; Ackerman 1998). The obvious question is: Why are women so prominent in the book?

Bledstein has suggested that the book as a whole is a satire, written by a woman, conceivably Huldah the prophet (Bledstein 1993). This is an extremely improbable thesis. First of all, as the previous chapters and the first part of this chapter have emphasized, the book is not a unity – we cannot speak of a single author of the book. In addition, most stories within the book show none of the indicators noted above (pp. 48–9 [in connection to Judges 13]) for stories that might be attributed to women. The story of Jephthah's daughter indicates just the opposite. The last few verses of chapter 11, which describe the yearly ritual to commemorate Jephthah's daughter, are very obscure; this may most likely be explained, I believe, by assuming that a man who only had an outsider's view of the ritual wrote them. I even suspect that much of the story concerning the daughter of Jephthah originated as an etiology written by a man for a women's ritual that he vaguely knew about, and was attempting to explain to his male audience. From the little we may piece together about gendered authorship in the Bible, Judges as a whole is not likely to be written by a woman (Brenner and van Dijk-Hemmes 1996).

Hackett offers a different type of solution to the prominence of women in Judges (Hackett 1987). She notes that the period of judges was a transitional period of instability, and based on historical analogies suggests that "women could fill leadership roles in this era of decentralized power and ad hoc leaders" (Hackett 1987: 156). This model might work within a scholarly framework that accepted the basic historicity of the period of judges. This is no longer the case, so the model must be rejected.

Other scholars have made claims about women's centrality without making the concomitant claims for either female authorship, or for the historicity Judges, in the belief that it derives from a period in which women really were powerful. Klein, for example, sees the book as playing off a paradigm established in the first chapter for Achsah (Klein 1993), but the themes she provides do not unify the book in a comprehensive fashion. The most compelling cases for viewing Judges as a women-centered book have been made by Bal.

Bal's *Death & Dissymmetry* is explicitly concerned with what keeps the book of Judges together, as its subtitle, *The Politics of Coherence in the Book of Judges* indicates. I agree with some of the theoretical underpinnings of the book, particularly with the way Bal asserts that Judges is "composed out of many sources ... [yet] conceived of as one text" (Bal 1988a: 4). Her major claim is that biblical scholars have been overly influenced by the political, which seems to be the explicit theme of the book. But that is not really the case. The real thesis is

> that the murders of young women in the book are caused by uncertainty about fatherhood – indeed, by the transition between an ancient and not very stable structure of kinship in which the daughter remains in her father's house and ... the virilocal, patrilineal one.
>
> (Bal 1988a: 6)

Most of Bal's book shows how readings of various episodes which focus on women fit this framework. Unfortunately, there is little evidence that the anthropological shift she indicates, which is the basis for the hypothesis, is accurate (Brettler 1990b). Furthermore, in her shift from coherence on the basis of political themes to coherence on the basis of social themes, she leaves out significant portions of the book, including, for example, the Ehud pericope. It would seem that any attempt to examine the book's coherence should at minimum be able to explain the present placement and structure of the major judges.

Bal and others have correctly noted that women are unusually significant in Judges. However, their use in the narrative forms no pattern, and women do not function as the basis of the coherence of Judges. Women play too many roles to form a coherent theme. Achsah's presence in chapter1 should not be exaggerated. Her presence there reflects that unit's quotation of Joshua in its effort to highlight Caleb. The concubine in Gibeah is highlighted as a type of parody of Sam 11:7, to create a world upside-down. The anonymous woman who kills Abimelech is there to deprecate Abimelech by having him killed by a woman – she is an agent, and doesn't approach a full-fledged character. The nameless woman with whom Samson is entangled in chapters 14–15 is a fleshed out foreign woman from Proverbs. Jephthah's daughter provides an opportunity to denigrate her father, the judge. Women are useful for characterizing the men around them. Many of the women function in this way – some are not much different than "Mrs. Job," who has a single line (2:9), which makes her husband look even better!

In sum, women are useful characters in Judges, helping to propel forward the plot of various stories. Their prominence does not mean that the book reflects a real period when women were strong, that it was written by a woman, or even by an author who had a particular interest in women. It does not indicate that the author was more interested in the social than in the political, since these women, as we shall see next, are deeply enmeshed in much of the activity of Judges, which is fundamentally political.

Judges as a Book

Especially when confronted with the diversity of material incorporated into Judges, and the fact that it is not organized in an obvious way, it is tempting to simply say that it is a collection of material that somehow came together to fill out the period between conquest and monarchy. It is easy to apply the model for the Samson pericope (pp. 58–60) to the book as a whole: various material was assembled in stages, and does not cohere. Thus, from a *modern* literary point of view we might speak of understanding the book as a whole, but this is inappropriate in a literary–historical framework, since a book was never structured into a whole; instead, various traditions were put into a chronological framework to fill out a period of time.

Though the treatment of the Samson pericope and the highlighting of the diversity of material incorporated in the book might suggest such an approach, internal evidence from the book itself suggests that it may not be viewed as a haphazard collection of material.[1]

Judges is constructed as a book, with an introduction and a conclusion.[2] As we saw above, the last five chapters should not be considered an appendix; they are integral to, and integrated into, the rest of the book. This is clearest, as noted, in the way that they both include notes saying "Judah shall ascend" (1:2; 20:18) and contain notices that everyone went home to their territory (2:6; 21:24). These correspondences and others are noted by Zakovitch, who feels that they are so strong it is likely that the introduction and conclusion were originally adjacent to each other (Zakovitch 1983: 175). This is unlikely; instead, an editor created these similarities to frame the work, to help create a book.

The evidence cited earlier about the odd correspondence between the end of the Samson unit and the beginning of the concubine of Gibeah unit, namely that both cite the unusual eleven hundred shekels of silver (16:5; 17:2; Zakovitch 1983: 169), suggests that chapters 17–21. should not be seen as an appendix. There are other similarities as well, including the fact that both of these episodes transpire in Dan, and specifically mention the cities Zorah and Eshtaol (13:25; 16:31; 18:2, 8, 11; Zakovitch 1983: 169).

The phrase used in 14:3 and 7 of the Philistine woman who was "pleasing" to Samson is unusual, but is identical to the phrase used in 17:6 and 21:25 to express that people did as they pleased (ישר + עין). Zakovitch suggests that these types of correspondences are due to the associative ordering of Judges: pericopae with similar themes and terms were placed adjacently, as elsewhere in the Bible. Although in some cases associative ordering or catch-lines may have influenced the placement of individual units in the Bible, its use as a general organizing principle by some scholars, including Zakovitch, is exaggerated (Levinson 1991: 14–35).

Yet, much of the material collected by Zakovitch concerning similarities between adjacent units in Judges is very compelling; he shows a significant number of verbal similarities between adjacent units. If it is unlikely that this material was original to both units, then these similarities must be explained by an editor or editors who created them by copying phrases between adjacent units. The similarities are then very significant, since they indicate that Judges should not be viewed as a haphazard collection of traditions, filling in the time period, but as a group of traditions that were smoothed together to create a book. The construction of these materials into a book goes beyond the stereotypical introductions and conclusions to each unit which allow the material to fill the time between conquest and monarchy.

A final, overlapping indication of the way in which these materials have been structured as a book concerns the order of tribes in the first and second sections of the book. Although the genres of the first part, the traditions about conquest and lack of conquest of the land, and the second part, about the judges, could not be more different, they both share the same ordering of the tribes, beginning with Judah, and ending with Dan (Globe 1990: 240–1). This tightly ties the first and second sections together.

These connections overlap. The inclusio ties the beginning to the end, creating a frame for the whole. The sequence of tribes ties the first part to the second part. Particularly strong literary reverberations connect the end of the second part to the third part. Similarities between adjacent units tie each episode to its neighbor. Though the traditions might be disparate in form, origin, and time of composition, they have been brought together as a book.

Long Live David!

The function of an introduction of a book is to introduce it – to give the reader a sense of its main themes, and of the author's perspective. A conclusion, as recapitulation, has a similar function. As we have already seen, the themes of the introduction and conclusion of Judges are very clear. As illustrated in Chapter Seven, the introduction emphasizes that Judah is the chosen tribe – it is given the most narrative space and, in contrast to the other tribes, succeeds in its mandate to conquer.

The significance of this pro-Judean theme is clarified in the conclusion, which dovetails with the introduction. The explicit theme of the final five chapters is kingship, as emphasized in its fourfold refrain, "In those days there was no king in Israel." The clear references to Saul with a (not so) "hidden polemic" anchor this theme more deeply. Thus, when put together, this framework is as clear in its purpose as the opening of 1 Chr 5:2, "Judah became more powerful than his brothers and a leader came from him."

The middle material has been structured to emphasize the same message. The episode of Othniel, the Judean Kenizzite who defeats "double-wickedness" was created as a model of an unambiguously positive Judean leader. The author/editor did not have a tradition or text that would serve this key function, so he made one up. The rest of the book, however, which does not share the stereotypical style of the Othniel episode, is comprised of traditions that (in a modified form) were organized and integrated into the book.

Two patterns intersect in the main section of Judges, concerning the major judges: a geographical pattern and an implicit value-judgmental pattern. The geographical pattern, recognized first by Malamat and noted above, is from South to North, from Judah to Dan (Globe 1990: 240–1). As the narrative moves to the North, the judges' behavior is more and more questionable.

Benjamin presented a particular problem for this author/editor, since according to tradition, Saul derived from Benjamin, yet the tribal allotment of Benjamin was often part of the Judean state. This second factor explains why the author chose as his second account a narrative which tells of the success of Ehud the Benjaminite. There is nothing in this story or in Ehud's genealogy or behavior that might connect him to Saul. In other words, he is being viewed as part of greater Judea, and the Ehud pericope and the concubine of Gibeah pericope should be read together: the "bad" Benjaminite is the one who comes from Gibeah, and rejects Ramah and

Jerusalem; otherwise, Benjaminites who have integrated into Judea and have proper allegiances are fine. Ehud is one such Benjaminite.

This reading of the Ehud story is very different from that proposed in Chapter Three, but the goal, or more precisely the framework within which the same story is being read, is very different at these two places in the same book. In Chapter Three, the emphasis was on the story itself, which likely existed in some form before Judges came together as a book. Yet, once we have shown that Judges is a book which has been consciously edited together, that same story gets a new meaning through this new framework and its relation to the rest of the book, namely that leadership from Judea rather than the northern kingdom is proper.

The final judges are just the opposite of Othniel and Ehud. This is especially clear for Samson, particularly in the final form of chapters 13–16, which might suggest that he has broken all of his Nazirite vows: he comes in contact with corpses and eats impurities (e.g. the honey from the lion's corpse), he goes to parties, where he likely drinks intoxicants, and he cuts his hair. Particularly if the editing of Judges should be seen as exilic or later, the fact that he is involved with foreign women is a serious offense. Within the broader context of Judges, Samson is a negative role model.

Jephthah is not much better. From the beginning he is introduced as "the son of a prostitute" (11:1). In his diplomatic negotiations in chapter 11, he cannot get his history right. He sacrifices his daughter. The last act recorded of him is killing forty-two thousand Ephraimites (12:6).

The Gideon–Abimelech material also provides negative models for northern judges. Gideon's career begins with his inability to recognize a divine messenger (6:11ff.). He asks for an excessive number of divine signs. He is too afraid to tear down the Baal altar by day, and secretly does this at night (6:27). He is vindictive against his countrymen (8:4–17). His final act is setting up an ephod (8:27). His son Abimelech is even worse, killing off his brothers (9:5). He deserves his shameful fate of being killed by a woman (9:53–4).

The case with Deborah–Barak is less clear-cut. Modern literature has emphasized the positive role of Deborah, and has forgotten that in the text she is paired with Barak, who would have been viewed negatively for agreeing to command a battle only if a woman came with him (4:8), even though he knew that the enemy would be handed to a woman (4:9). Deborah is not a full-fledged judge; the text offers no commissioning story for her, and has no death notice. Thus, although she certainly is not as problematic as Gideon, Abimelech, Jephthah and Samson, she is not as unambiguously positive as the two first Judean major judges.

A clear pattern falls into place, which mirrors chapter 1:It is the Judean judges who are unambiguously good, and the northern leaders who are bad. Noting that the judges, like the tribes in chapter 1, are described geographically, from south to north, is not sufficient – it is crucial to realize that this geographical patterning is connected to a set of value judgements, as in chapter 1.

Material concerning Ephraim in 8:1–3 and 12:1–6 seconds this pattern. In both cases, Ephraim acts inappropriately. As Globe notes, in these contexts "Ephraim [is] a synonym for the later northern kingdom of Israel" (Globe 1990: 234). It is not only through a description of its negative behavior that Ephraim, namely the northern kingdom, is chastised, but even through the placement of Ephraim out of geographical order in a section that is otherwise so ordered – this suggests that Ephraim is destabilizing (Globe 1990: 249–50). It is thus quite clear that the South–North pattern which matches the good–bad pattern in both the book's introduction and main section argues "not only for the necessity of a king, but elliptically for the Judean monarchy" (Globe 1990: 234).

Globe might even be understating the case when he suggests that this argument is elliptic, that it is a type of what Amit might call a "hidden polemic." The message is doubly doubled in the first sixteen chapters of the book – the patterns of chapter 1 and chapters 3–16 mirror each other, and the doubling of the Ephraim episode makes sure that the reader will not miss its point. This doubling is similar to the inclusion of two stories in the Saul–David narrative about how David had an opportunity to kill Saul but did not (1 Samuel 24 and 26), a story which helps to clear David of the possible accusation that he was a usurper who wanted Saul dead (Brettler 1995: 104). Editors most likely collected and included doubled traditions to make a clear point which should not be ignored.

This pro-Judean, anti-non-Davidic kingship bias of the book continues throughout the end of the book. Chapter Six highlighted the anti-Saul, pro-Judean bias of the final episode of Judges. Amit has shown in great detail the various polemical elements in Judges 17–18 which mock the religious system of the north (Amit 2000: 99–118). This is a final argument for not reading the last five chapters as an appendix; in contrast, e.g. to the appendix to Samuel (Brueggemann 1988), which disagrees with the previous chapters of that book, the final five chapters of Judges "third" a theme which has already been seconded.

This section has developed a political reading of Judges as a whole. This way of approaching the book was suggested independently from several different perspectives by several scholars in the late 1980s and early 1990s (Stone 1988; Amit 1999; Brettler 1989a). O'Connell agrees that the "implicit rhetorical purpose" of the book is "idealizing the monarchy of Judah" (O'Connell 1996: 268). Sweeney introduces one of the most recent studies of this issue with the following observation:

> A major shift is now taking place in the study of the book of Judges as scholars have come to recognize that the book must no longer be read simply as an historical source that reflects the historical and social realities of pre-monarchic Israel. Judges must also be read as a literary work that presents a specific socio-political and religious understanding of Israel in the pre-monarchic period in keeping with the historiographical interests of its composer. An important dimension of this discussion is the recognition that Judges presents a polemical view of early Israelite history that promotes the interests of the tribe of Judah and the Davidic dynasty ... .
>
> (Sweeney 1997: 517)

This book has been an attempt to show, building on the insights of others, how the author/editor of Judges achieves this goal by taking earlier traditions and texts, modifying them slightly, adding new texts, and recontextualizing the old so this message comes through.

This message is conveyed through the structure of the book of Judges as a whole. This explains why there are some sections of the book which, as far as I can tell, do not serve this purpose. I do not see how the minor judges fit in, and can only offer one of the standard biblical scholarship answers – it was traditional material that an editor included, or someone inserted it after the book already took shape – but these answers are not verifiable and are not really satisfactory. Furthermore, there was some attempt to make Judges fit in better with the broader Dtr corpus. Judges is not a typical Dtr book (but what is?); like Samuel, but unlike Kings and some parts of Joshua, it is not infused with Dtr terminology and ideology. It emphasizes God's grace in raising up the Judges –

Israel need not repent for YHWH to raise up the judge (Greenspahn 1986). The one exception is at the center of the book, in 10:10, where the Israelites confess "We have sinned against you." This theological scene is secondary to the major *Tendenz* of the book, and is most likely a late Dtr addition.

I do not mean to create a dichotomy between politics and theology. Certainly, in ancient Israel, as in the rest of the ancient near eastern world, people believed that kings reigned through the power of various deities. This is particularly clear in the Assyrian royal inscriptions and palace reliefs (Porter 1993: 138–43). Texts like 2 Samuel 7, and Psalms 89 and 132 illustrate the intertwining of politics and theology in Israel. Thus, when I claim that the work is predominantly political, I do not mean to downplay the theological aspect of Israelite politics; I do, however, mean to suggest that its primary purpose was not theological in some other sense that is divorced from the issue of: Whom did YHWH choose as the legitimate king?

There are many plausible time periods when such a message would have been necessary. Judg 18:30 clearly dates from after the exile of the Northern kingdom, and if this is original to the book, then the entire book would need to be from the end of the eighth century or later. Some evidence was explored in Chapter Four, suggesting that part of the Samson material is exilic or later. In any case, just as the desire for kingship by the Saulides did not die when David reigned, it is highly unlikely that desire for northern kingship died with that exile. The exilic Ezek 37:15–28 indicates that northern Israelites with royal ambitions existed through the exilic period. Thus, a wide variety of scenarios, pre-exilic, exilic, post-exilic, Babylonian or in the land of Israel, could be imagined for when the book with its strong pro-Davidic political message might have come together.

It is equally impossible to decide exactly how many stages of editing the book went through, and at what point it became a political work. Until we better understand how much tension might be incorporated into a single-authored work, and the extent to which a single author might vary his formulae, we will be at a stalemate in determining layers of redaction.

This political reading closely associates Judges with the following Book of Samuel, rather than the previous Book of Joshua, to which it is more traditionally connected. In fact, Judges, with its strong anti-Saul bias, should be seen as a prefiguration of Samuel; its strong anti-North bias connects it to Kings. Prefiguration is an important tool of the biblical historian (Brettler 1995: 48–61), and its use here should be seen within the broader biblical use of this device.

This book, and this chapter, have made several claims about the purposes of both individual units and the book of Judges as a whole. It is notoriously difficult to evaluate such claims, yet they should not be viewed as pure conjectures. My goal has been to explain the book of Judges as it is currently structured, to construct a background which "offers a critically plausible account of the texts as relics of the past" (Davies 1987: 10). This background will need to be weighed against other backgrounds in terms of the extent to which it succeeds in explaining the current shape of Judges given what we know about ancient Israelite society. Given what we know about ancient Israel, Judges is not a book of history in the sense of a work interested in the real past, nor is it work of literature in the sense of *belles lettres*. Instead, it is a highly political work, which echoes the following sentiment, found elsewhere in the Bible (1 Kgs 1:31): "May my lord King David live forever!"

NOTES

PREFACE

1 English translations typically follow the NJPS version, though this is often modified.

1 JUDGES AND THE HISTORIAN

1 There is no paraphrase of the Othniel story in 3:7–11; contrast Bright, and the treatment of Malamat discussed below.
2 A European analogy would be Portugal arriving first to help Germany.
3 This type of methodology is often associated with W.F. Albright, and is criticized at great length by the Copenhagen school, especially Thomas L. Thompson (Thompson 1992: 11–26, esp. 17). Moles, a classicist, comments sharply on the problem of "extract[ing] factual material from an ancient historiographical text," comparing it to messy surgery (Moles 1993: 114).
4 The crisis raised or embodied in this History may be seen in the reviews and reactions edited by Philip R. Davies and David M. Gunn (Davies and Gunn 1987: 3–63). For a more recent survey on this issue, see Lester L. Grabbe's *Can A "History of Israel" Be Written?* (Grabbe 1997).
5 See my forthcoming "The Copenhagen School: The Historiographical Issues."

2 READING JUDGES AS LITERATURE?

1 This chapter had its genesis at the seminar on Bible and Literature at Indiana University; it was then presented at a student-faculty seminar at the University of Chicago, at the 1999 International SBL meeting in Finland and at the colloquium on the Hebrew Bible of the Boston Theological Institute. Many people have helped shape the arguments developed here.
2 For an early analysis of the opposite pulls of reading the Bible as history and as literature, see James Barr, "Reading the Bible as Literature" (Barr 1973b: 20–30).

3 For earlier critiques of the Bible as literature, see James Kugel, "On the Bible and Literary Criticism" (Kugel 1981b) and "James Kugel Responds" (Kugel 1982), and John Barton, "Reading the Bible as Literature: Two Questions for Biblical Critics" (Barton 1987).

4 An important earlier work arguing for the use of literary methods was the SBL presidential address of James Muilenburg (Muilenburg 1969); this essay and others reflecting "rhetorical criticism" are reprinted in Thomas F. Best's *Hearing and Speaking the Word: Selections from the Works of James Muilenburg* (Best 1984). Important early work was published in Spanish by Luis Alonso Schökel, and in modern Hebrew by Meir Sternberg and Menakhem Perry, but these influenced few scholars.

5 The diagram in the book is in Hebrew; I have used my own English translation in an attempt to highlight the chiastic parallels.

6 Professor David P. Wright of Brandeis University, who heard this paper at the Boston Theological Institute colloquium, suggested calling this chiastic interference.

7 Professor Herb Marks of Indiana University encouraged me to formulate the distinction in this way.

8 Seven of the eleven uses of the term in the Hebrew Bible appear in these chapters.

9 There is a tremendous need to write the equivalent of Barbara Herrnstein Smith's *Poetic Closure* (Smith 1968) for biblical studies.

10 Garsiel's point is made via a diagram on pp. 128–9. The diagrams constructed by literary scholars are often very obtuse.

11 David M. Gunn concludes with reflections on the possibility of "a rapprochement between the old and the new," by which he meant the historical critical and literary methods; but he saw the two traveling on "separate roads for a long way ahead," and was not very sorry, because "historical critical inquiry does not make much contribution" to literary study (Gunn 1987: 73).

12 Chronicles, for example, was often belittled as a late work of little literary merit, but has been the subject of at least two book-length literary studies: Rodney K. Duke, *The Persuasive Appeal of the Chronicler: A Rhetorical Analysis* (Duke 1990), and Isaac Kalimi, *The Book of Chronicles: Historical Writing and Literary Devices* (Kalimi 2000).

13 Literary competence is a major theme of John Barton, *Reading the Old Testament: Method in Biblical Study* (Barton 1996).

14 The approach I am advocating, however, must maintain double disciplinary focus and integrity; otherwise it will be criticized legitimately as "lazy eclecticism," which is seen all too often in our field (Barton 1994: 3–15; Joyce 1994: 17–27).

3 THE SHORT STORY

1 Throughout this study, I follow convention and use the word "judge" as a translation of the Hebrew שֹׁפֵט, even though this is not accurate (Boling 1975: 5–7; Soggin 1981: 104).

2 The stories of the major judges have Dtr additions at their beginnings and ends, incorporating them into chronological narrative that fits the

paradigm offered in 2:11–19. Thus, when I speak of composite units, I refer to units whose middle section, outside of the framework, is composite.

3 It is uncertain whether the Jephthah story material (10:6 or 11:1–12:7) is a unified composition, and thus if it should be read as a short story or a cycle (Richter 1966: 485–556).

4 There is some debate concerning the exact form of the structure, as well as whether or not it is Dtr (Lindars 1995: 98–101).

5 The understanding of the creative roles of editors or redactors in reshaping texts, and thus functioning as authors, has come to be appreciated in the last few decades by biblical scholars, and is reflected in the term "author–editor" (O'Connell 1996).

6 I am assuming that 3:31 is later than 10:11 (O'Connell 1996: 345–68).

7 The definite article is present in Hebrew, but it remains unclear when this must be translated as "the" (GKC §126q-s; Barr 1989a: 307–35).

8 See e.g. Deut 6:12; 8:11, 14, 19; 1 Sam 12:9.

9 See Judg 6:2, but in a different sense.

10 It is likely that Judges 1 knew some form of Joshua (Brettler 1989c).

11 The role of rhyme in biblical texts is overemphasized by Watson (Watson 1986: 229–34).

12 The following section is a revision of *The Creation of History in Ancient Israel* (Brettler 1995: 79–90), which was based on "Never the Twain Shall Meet? The Ehud Story as History and Literature" (Brettler 1991: 285–304). The extensive notes found there have been omitted, except for the cases of direct quotation and citation. Some literature that has been written after the chapter of *The Creation of History* was completed has been added (Lindars 1995: 127–56; Amit 1999: 171–98; O'Connell 1996: 84–100).

13 The translation anticipates my understanding of the pericope's genre and purpose, and in this case, diverges noticeably from the NJPS.

14 Alternately, "were more evil than before."

15 An idiom for urinating; note the repeated use of a body part.

16 אחלי! תבוא לי ויבוא הנצב אחר הלהב (Yellin 1934: 130–1). Some sense of Abulafiah's concern with love and his explicit use of sexual imagery is seen in the selection of his poems in *The Penguin Book of Hebrew Verse* (Carmi 1981: 410–16). I would like to thank Mr Noah Feldman for calling this poem to my attention.

17 Stephen Geller called this to my attention.

18 On humor in the Bible, see *On Humour and the Comic in the Hebrew Bible* (Radday and Brenner 1990). Bruce William Jones raises issues concerning humor in Esther that are directly applicable to our passage in Judges (Jones 1977). On the function of humor within religion, see *Humor and Laughter: An Anthropological Approach* (Apte 1985: 151–76). Specifically on satire and religion, see *All Things Vain: Religious Satirists and Their Art* (Kantra 1984).

19 Webb, like Alter, does not adequately explore the social dynamics of this satire.

20 E.g. שיר and תודה (Kraus 1988: 38–62; cf. Feininger 1981: 91–103, esp. 97–8).

21 Hobsbawm and Ranger adduce modern cases of such inventions. These cases serve as important illustrations of how quickly falsehoods are believed and of the social mechanisms involved in the creation of new traditions. This essay has been especially influential in biblical studies.

22 Some specific examples of the misuse of this story by modern historians of ancient Israel are cited in *The Creation of History in Ancient Israel* (Brettler 1995: 88).

23 See above, p. 17. O'Connell (O'Connell 1996: 84), among others, generalizes the attitude toward Eglon to reflect foreign kingship in general; this goes beyond the evidence of the text.

4 THE SAMSON CYCLE

1 The Book of Chronicles offers important examples of inconsistencies within a single-authored book (Kalimi 2000: 363–84).

2 As noted by Barrera, the manuscript does, however, have important points of contact with the Greek proto-Lucianic text of Judges, and that text might, with care, now play a more significant role in our understanding of the recensions of Judges (Barrera 1989).

3 Alternately, "were more evil than before."

4 See Judg 17:1; 1 Sam 1:1; 9:1, and the LBH variant in Job 1:1.

5 Amit discusses the history of scholarship of this verse, citing some scholars who do not feel that it indicates the later authorship of what follows (Amit 1999: 266 n. 54).

6 Note that the only other uses of פעם with רוח are in the late Dan 2:1, 3, and in Gen 41:8 (Brettler 1995: 180 n. 73).

7 *OTP* 2.255–6 (= *L.A.B.* 42).

8 In fact, the title of Yairah Amit, "'Manoah Promptly Followed his Wife' (Judges 13.11): On the Place of the Woman in Birth Narratives," (Amit 1993), is taken from this verse. This article offers an important analysis of Manoah's characterization.

9 The debate concerning the exact identification of this animal need not concern us.

10 A different group of Proverbs, however, emphasizes the importance of human preparation for war, and seems to leave YHWH out of the picture (e.g. 20:18; 24:6).

11 I am intentionally playing on Robert Alter's term of "historicized prose fiction" (Alter 1981: 27).

12 The force of the imperative is blunted in most translations.

13 Cases where it is very likely editorial are 2 Sam 2:1; 8:1; 10:1; 13:1 and 2 Kgs 6:24. It is used within a single story in 1 Sam 24:6.

14 Most scholars divide Ruth into the four parts reflected in the chapter headings. However, the use of noun-first disjunctives in chapters 2 and 4, but not chapter 3, might suggest that the structure is chapters 1, 2–3, 4.

15 This has some striking parallels to the Suffering Servant material in Isaiah, most likely from approximately the same time.

16 Exum overstates, however, when she claims (p. 42) that "The one who answers prayer is the true center of attention in each cycle."

5 POETRY AND PROSE IN JUDGES 4–5

1 28:6; 31:22; 41:14; 72:18; 89:53; 106:48; 124:6; 135:21; 144:1.
2 See 2 Sam 11:21. There have been many studies of the images of women in Judges 4 and 5 (Bal 1988b; 1989: 50–132; van der Kooij 1996: 136–52; van Wolde 1996: 283–95; G.P. Miller 1998: 126; Ackerman 1998: 27–88).
3 Coincidentally (?) this is a theme of the Gideon unit, which immediately follows; see esp. 6:15.
4 On the meaning of נדב, see *HALOT* 2.671; for cases where עם is used of a military unit, see *HALOT* 2.838, 3d. See also v. 9.
5 The evidence cited by Jacob Milgrom may be turned on its head (Milgrom 1982).
6 This title is taken from Halpern (Halpern 1983a: 41–73).
7 Future references to Halpern are to his revision of this article in *The First Historians*.
8 I ask this as a historical question, in contrast to Danna Nolan Fewell and David M. Gunn (Fewell and Gunn 1990), who are interested in the literary question of how we might *read* both chapters together.

6 WINDING DOWN: THE CONCUBINE OF GIBEAH

1 Isaiah 36–9 might be similar, but is more complex.
2 The focus of this chapter is Judges 19. I do not mean to imply, like Hans-Winfried Jüngling (Jüngling 1981), that this chapter may be totally separated in terms of composition from chapters 20–1.
3 It is noteworthy that the Jephthah pericope is also treated by her; two of her four central texts of terror are from Judges!
4 The reading of Michael Carden, though very different than Trible, is similar in this regard. Note especially: "I must acknowledge that my intent is also to detoxify Genesis 19 and Judges 19–21 as texts of terror for queer people" (Carden 1999: 85).
5 The following notes on chapter 19 are only tentative, and are meant to be suggestive rather than comprehensive and conclusive. The expression היא ירושלם is found in Judg 19:10 and 1 Chr 11:4. Explicitly defining the נכרי as not from ישראל is found in v. 12, and in 1 Kgs 8:41, 43, which are considered exilic (Brettler 1993: 17–35). In BH, "the old person" is usually expressed as זקן; for האיש הזקן (v. 20), compare (in the plural) Ezek 9:6. Finally, the two expressions כל הלילה עד הבקר (v. 25) and נתח ל (v. 29) are only found in priestly literature (Exod 29:17; Lev 1:6, 12; 8:20).
6 Reading the standard meaning of זנה, with MT.

7 A CONCLUSION THAT BECAME AN INTRODUCTION

1 The reason why I disagree with other scholars who claim that 1:1–3:6 is a two-part introduction, whose first part ends with 2:10, will become clear in this chapter.

2 This section is a revision of my "Jud 1,1–2,10: From Appendix to Prologue" (Brettler 1989c). The notes of that article have not been reproduced here.

3 Josh 24:32–3 are later additions made in an attempt to create a Persian Hexateuch (Brettler and Römer 2000: 408–16).

8 CONCLUSION: THE CENTER DOES COHERE

1 Much of the material in the rest of this chapter is a revision of "The Book of Judges: Literature as Politics" (Brettler 1989a). Complete footnotes and references may be found there.

2 I do not find compelling the argument of Sweeney for a two-part structure for the book (Sweeney 1997).

REFERENCES

Ackerman, S. (1998) *Warrior, Dancer, Seductress, Queen: Women in Judges and Biblical Israel*, AB Reference Library, New York: Doubleday.

Ackroyd, P.R. (1952) "The Composition of the Song of Devorah," *VT* 2: 160–2.

—— (1971) *The First Book of Samuel*, CBC, Cambridge: Cambridge University Press.

Ahlström, G.W. (1977) "Judges 5:20 f. and History," *JNES* 36:287–8.

—— (1993) *The History of Ancient Palestine from the Paleolithic Period to Alexander's Conquest*, JSOTSup 146, Sheffield: Sheffield Academic Press.

Albertz, R. (1994) *A History of Israelite Religion in the Old Testament Period*, Philadelphia: Westminster/John Knox.

Albright, W.F. (1922) "The Earliest Forms of Hebrew Verse," *Journal of the Palestine Oriental Society* 2:69–86.

—— (1936) "The Song of Deborah in the Light of Archaeology," *BASOR* 62:26–31.

Alonso-Schökel, L. (1961) "Erzählkunst im Buche der Richter," *Bib* 42:149–57.

Alter, R. (1981) *The Art of Biblical Narrative*, New York: Basic Books.

—— (1983) "How Conventions Help Us Read: The Case of the Bible's Annunciation Type-Scene," *Prooftexts* 3:115–30.

—— (1985) *The Art of Biblical Poetry*, New York: Basic Books.

Amit, Y. (1987) "The Dual Causality Principle and Its Effects on Biblical Literature," *VT* 37:385–400.

—— (1993) "'Manoah Promptly Followed His Wife' (Judges 13.11): On the Place of the Woman in Birth Narratives," in A. Brenner (ed.) *A Feminist Companion to Judges*, Feminist Companion to the Bible 4, Sheffield: JSOT Press.

—— (1999) *The Book of Judges: The Art of Editing*, trans. J. Chipman, Biblical Interpretation Series 38, Leiden: Brill.

—— (2000) *Hidden Polemics in Biblical Narrative*, Biblical Interpretation Series 25, Leiden: Brill.

Anderson, A.A. (1981) *Psalms*, NCB, Grand Rapids, MI: Eerdmans.

Anderson, B. (1978) "From Analysis to Synthesis: The Interpretation of Genesis 1–11," *JBL* 97:23–39.

Apte, M.L. (1985) *Humor and Laughter: An Anthropological Approach*, Ithaca: Cornell University Press.

Auld, A.G. (1975) "Judges I and History: A Reconsideration," *VT* 25:261–85. Reprinted in A.G. Auld (1998) *Joshua Retold: Synoptic Perspectives*, Edinburgh: T & T Clark.

Bal, M. (1987) *Lethal Love: Literary Feminist Interpretations of Biblical Lovestories*, Bloomington: Indiana University Press.

—— (1988a) *Death & Dissymmetry: The Politics of Coherence in the Book of Judges*, Chicago: University of Chicago Press.

—— (1988b) *Murder and Difference: Genre, Gender and Scholarship on Sisera's Death*, Bloomington: Indiana University Press.

—— (ed.) (1989) *Anti-Covenant: Counter-Reading Women's Lives in the Hebrew Bible*, JSOTSup 81, Bible and Literature Series 22, Sheffield: Almond.

—— (1993) "A Body of Writing: Judges 19," in A. Brenner (ed.) *A Feminist Companion to Judges*, Feminist Companion to the Bible 4, Sheffield: JSOT Press.

Barr, J. (1973a) *The Bible in the Modern World*, New York: Harper & Row.

—— (1973b) "Reading the Bible as Literature," *BJRL* 56:1–30.

—— (1989a) "Determination and the Definite Article in Biblical Hebrew," *JSS* 34:307–35.

—— (1989b) "The Literal, the Allegorical, and Modern Biblical Scholarship," *JSOT* 44:3–17.

Barrera, T.J. (1989) "Textual Variants in 4QJudg^a and the Textual and Editorial History of the Book of Judges," *RevQ* 14/54:229–45.

Barton, J. (1987) "Reading the Bible as Literature: Two Questions for Biblical Critics," *Journal of Literature and Theology* 1:135–53.

—— (1994) "Historical Criticism and Literary Interpretation: Is There Any Common Ground?" in S. Porter *et al.* (eds) *Crossing the Boundaries: Essays in Biblical Interpretation in Honour of Michael D. Goulder*, Biblical Interpretation Series 8, Leiden: Brill.

—— (1996) *Reading the Old Testament: Method in Biblical Study*, revised and enlarged edition, Louisville, KY: Westminster/John Knox.

Bellis, A.O. (1994) *Helpmates, Harlots, and Heroes: Women's Stories in the Hebrew Bible*, Louisville, KY: Westminster/John Knox.

Berlin, A. (1983) *Poetics and Interpretation of Biblical Narrative*, Bible and Literature Series, Sheffield: Almond.

Best, T.F. (1984) *Hearing and Speaking the Word: Selections from the Works of James Muilenburg*, Chico, CA: Scholars.

Bickerman, E. (1967) *Four Strange Books of the Bible*, New York: Schocken.

Bird, P.A. (1997) *Missing Persons and Mistaken Identities: Women and Gender in Ancient Israel*, OBT, Minneapolis: Fortress.

Bledstein, A.J. (1993) "Is Judges a Women's Satire of Men Who Played God?" in A. Brenner (ed.) *A Feminist Companion to Judges*, Feminist Companion to the Bible 4, Sheffield: JSOT Press.

Blenkinsopp, J. (1961) "Ballad Style and Psalm Style in the Song of Deborah: A Discussion," *Bib* 42:61–76.

—— (1963) "Structure and Style in Judges 13–16," *JBL* 82:65–76.

—— (1991) "The Social Context of the 'Outsider Woman' in Proverbs 1–9," *Bib* 72:457–73.

Boda, M.J. (1996) "Chiasmus in Ubiquity: Symmetrical Mirages in Nehemiah 9," *JSOT* 71:55–70.

Boling, R.G. (1975) *Judges*, AB 6A, Garden City, NY: Doubleday.

Bowersock, G.W. (1994) *Fiction as History: Nero to Julian*, Berkeley: Univeristy of California Press.

Brenner, A. (1990) "A Triangle and a Rhombus in Narrative Structure: A Proposed Integrative Reading of Judges IV and V," *VT* 40:129–38.

—— (ed.) (1993a) *A Feminist Companion to Judges*, Feminist Companion to the Bible 4, Sheffield: JSOT Press.

—— (1993b) *A Feminist Companion to Ruth*, Feminist Companion to the Bible 3, Sheffield: Sheffield Academic Press.

—— (1999) *Judges: A Feminist Companion to the Bible*, Feminist Companion to the Bible, Second Series, 4, Sheffield: Sheffield Academic Press.

Brenner, A. and van Dijk-Hemmes, F. (1996) *On Gendering Texts: Female and Male Voices in the Hebrew Bible*, Biblical Interpretation Series 1, Leiden: Brill.

Brett, M. (1990) "Four or Five Things to Do with Texts: A Taxonomy of Interpretive Interests," in D.J.A Clines *et al.* (eds) *The Bible in Three Dimensions: Essays in Celebration of Forty Years of Biblical Studies in the University of Sheffield*, JSOTSup 87, Sheffield: JSOT Press.

Brettler, M.Z. (1989a) "The Book of Judges: Literature as Politics," *JBL* 108:395–418.

—— (1989b) *God is King: Understanding an Israelite Metaphor*, JSOTSup 76, Sheffield: Sheffield Academic Press.

—— (1989c) "Jud 1,1–2,10: From Appendix to Prologue," *ZAW* 101:433–5.

—— (1990a) "Review of Halpern, *The First Historians*," *JR* 70:83–4.

—— (1990b) "Review of Bal *Death and Dissymmetry: The Politics of Coherence in the Book of Judges* and *Murder and Difference: Gender, Genre, and Scholarship on Sisera's Death*," *Hebrew Studies* 31:96–101.

—— (1991) "Never the Twain Shall Meet? The Ehud Story as History and Literature," *HUCA* 62:285–304.

—— (1993) "Interpretation and Prayer: Notes on the Composition of 1 Kings 8.15–53," in M. Brettler and M. Fishbane (eds) *Minḥah le-Naḥum*, JSOTSup 154, Sheffield: Sheffield Academic Press.

—— (1995) *The Creation of History in Ancient Israel*, London: Routledge.

—— (1997) "The Composition of 1 Samuel 1–2," *JBL* 116:601–12.

—— (forthcoming) "The Copenhagen School: The Historiographical Issues."

Brettler, M.Z. and Römer, T.C. (2000) "Deuteronomy 34 and the Case for a Persian Hexateuch," JBL 119:401–19.

Bright, J. (1981) *A History of Israel*, 3rd edition, Philadelphia: Westminster.

Brueggemann, W. (1988) "2 Samuel 21–24: An Appendix of Deconstruction?" *CBQ* 50:383–97.

Burney, C.F. (1970) *The Book of Judges with Introduction and Notes*, New York: Ktav.

Butterworth, M. (1992) *Structure and the Book of Zechariah*, JSOTSup 130, Sheffield: Sheffield Academic Press.

Camp, C. (1981) "What's So Strange About the Strange Woman?" in D. Jobling *et al.* (eds) *The Bible and the Politics of Exegesis: Essays in Honor of Norman K. Gottwald on his Sixty-fifth Birthday,* Cleveland: Pilgrim.

—— (1985) *Wisdom and the Feminine in the Book of Proverbs,* Bible and Literature Series 11, Sheffield: Almond.

—— (1987) "Woman Wisdom as Root Metaphor: A Theological Consideration," in K.G. Hoglund *et al.* (eds) *The Listening Heart: Essays in Wisdom and the Psalms in Honor of Roland E. Murphy, O. Carm,* JSOTSup 58, Sheffield: JSOT Press.

Caquot, A. (1986) "Les Tribus d'Israël dans le Cantique de Débora (Juges 5, 13–17)," *Semeia* 36:47–70.

Carden, M. (1999) "Homophobia and Rape in Sodom and Gibeah: A Response to Ken Stone," *JSOT* 82:83–96.

Carmi, T. (ed.) (1981) *The Penguin Book of Hebrew Verse,* New York: Viking.

Carr, D. (1996) *Reading the Fractures of Genesis: Historical and Literary Approaches,* Louisville, KY: Westminster/John Knox.

Carroll, R.P. (1986) *Jeremiah,* OTL, Philadelphia: Westminster.

—— (1993) "The Hebrew Bible as Literature – A Misprision?" *Studia Theologica* 47:77–90.

—— (1997) "Clio and Canons: In Search of a Cultural Poetics of the Hebrew Bible," *BibInt* 5:300–23.

Childs, B.S. (1967) *Isaiah and the Assyrian Crisis,* SBT^2 3, London: SCM.

Cogan, M. and Tadmor, H. (1988) *II Kings,* AB 11, New York: Doubleday.

Cohen, R. (1986) "History and Genre," *NLH* 17:203–18.

Cohen, D. (1989) "Fictional *versus* Historical Lives: Borderlines and Borderline Cases," *Journal of Narrative Techniques* 19:3–24.

Coogan, M.D. (1978) "A Structural and Literary Analysis of the Song of Deborah," *CBQ* 40:143–66.

Coxon, P.W. (1999) "Nephilim," in K. van der Toorn *et al.* (eds) *Dictionary of Deities and Demons in the Bible,* 2nd edition, Leiden: Brill.

Craigie, P.C. (1969) "The Song of Deborah and the Epic of Tukulti-Ninurta," *JBL* 88:253–65.

Crenshaw, J. (ed.) (1976) *Studies in Ancient Israelite Wisdom,* New York: Ktav.

—— (1978) *Samson: A Secret Betrayed, A Vow Ignored,* Atlanta: John Knox.

Davies, P.R. (1987) *Behind the Essenes: History and Ideology in the Dead Sea Scrolls,* BJS 94, Atlanta: Scholars.

—— (1998) *Scribes and Schools: The Canonization of the Hebrew Scriptures,* Library of Ancient Israel, Louisville, KY: Westminster/John Knox.

Davies, P.R. and Gunn, D.M. (eds) (1987) "A History of Ancient Israel and Judah: A Discussion of Miller-Hayes (1986)," *JSOT* 39:3–63.

de Moor, J.C. (ed.) (1995) *Synchronic or Diachronic? A Debate on Method in Old Testament Exegesis,* OTS 34, Leiden: Brill.

de Vaux, R. (1978) *The Early History of Israel,* Philadelphia: Westminster.

Dever, W.G. (1990) *Recent Archaeological Discoveries and Biblical Research,* Seattle: University of Washington Press.

Driver, S.R. (1972) *An Introduction to the Literature of the Old Testament,* Gloucester, MA: Peter Smith.

Duke, R.K. (1990) *The Persuasive Appeal of the Chronicler: A Rhetorical Analysis*, JSOTSup 88, Sheffield: Almond.

Edelman, D.V. (1991) *King Saul in the Historiography of Judah*, JSOTSup 121, Sheffield: Sheffield Academic Press.

Eliot, T.S. (1936) *Essays Ancient and Modern*, New York: Harcourt Brace.

Exum, J.C. (1981) "Aspects of Symmetry and Balance in the Samson Saga," *JSOT* 19:3–29.

—— (1983) "The Theological Dimensions of the Samson Saga," *VT* 33:3–45.

—— (1990) "The Centre Cannot Hold: Thematic and Textual Instabilities in Judges," *CBQ* 52:410–31.

—— (1993) *Fragmented Women: Feminist (Sub)versions of Biblical Narratives*, JSOTSup 163, Sheffield: Sheffield Academic Press.

—— (1995) "Feminist Criticism: Whose Interests are Being Served?" in G.A. Yee (ed.) *Judges and Method: New Approaches in Biblical Studies*, Minneapolis: Fortress.

Exum, J.C. and Clines, D.J.A. (eds) (1993) *The New Literary Criticism and the Hebrew Bible*, JSOTSup 143, Sheffield: JSOT Press.

Exum, J.C. and Whedbee, J.W. (1984) "Isaac, Samson, and Saul: Reflections on the Comic and the Tragic Visions," *Semeia* 32:5–40.

Febvre, L. (1973) *A New Kind of History and Other Essays*, Peter Burke (ed.) trans. K. Folca, New York: Harper & Row.

Feinberg, L. (1972) "Satire and Humor: In the Orient and in the West," *Costerus* 2:33–61.

Feininger, B. (1981) "A Decade of German Psalm–Criticism," *JSOT* 20:91–103.

Fewell, D.N. and Gunn, D.M. (1990) "Controlling Perspectives: Women, Men, and the Authority of Violence in Judges 4 & 5," *JAAR* 58:389–411.

—— (1991) "Tipping the Balance: Sternberg's Reader and the Rape of Dinah," *JBL* 110:193–211.

Finkelstein, I. and Na'aman, N. (eds) (1994) *From Nomadism to Monarchy: Archaeological and Historical Aspects of Early Israel*, Jerusalem: Israel Exporation Society.

Finnegan, R. (1977) *Oral Literature: Its Nature, Significance and Social Context*, Cambridge: Cambridge University Press.

Fishbane, M. (1985) *Biblical Interpretation in Ancient Israel*, Oxford: Oxford University Press.

Fletcher, A. (1964) *Allegory: The Theory of a Symbolic Mode,* Ithaca: Cornell University Press.

Fokkelman, J.P. (1975) *Narrative Art in Genesis*, Assen: van Gorcum.

—— (1981–93) *Narrative Art and Poetry in the Books of Samuel*, 4 vols, Assen: Van Gorcum.

—— (1999) *Reading Biblical Narrative: An Introductory Guide*, Louisville, KY: Westminster/John Knox.

Fornara, C.W. (1983) *The Nature of History in Ancient Greece and Rome*, Berkeley: University of California Press.

Foster, B.R. (1974) "Humor and Cuneiform Literature," *JANESCU* 6:69–85.

Fowler, J.D. (1988) *Theophoric Personal Names in Ancient Hebrew: A Comparative Study*, JSOTSup 49, Sheffield: Sheffield Academic Press.

Freedman, D.N. (1980) *Pottery, Poetry, and Prophecy: Collected Essays on Hebrew Poetry*, Winona Lake, IN: Eisenbrauns.

Fretz, M.J. and Panitz, R.I. (1992) "Caleb," *ABD* 1:808–10.

Frick, F.S. (1985) *The Formation of the State in Ancient Israel*, SWBAS 4, Sheffield: Almond.

Frye, N. (1957) *Anatomy of Criticism*, Princeton: Princeton University Press.

Frye, P. (1986) "Satire," in A. Preminger (ed.) *The Princeton Handbook of Poetic Terms,* Princeton: Princeton University Press.

Garsiel, M. (1985) *The First Book of Samuel: A Literary Study of Comparative Structures, Analogies and Parallels*, Ramat-Gan: Revivim.

Geller, S. (1982) "Theory and Method in the Study of Biblical Poetry," *JQR* 73:65–77.

—— (1996) *Sacred Enigmas: Literary Religion in the Hebrew Bible*, London: Routledge.

Gerleman, G. (1951) "The Song of Deborah in the Light of Stylistics," *VT* 1:168–80.

Gevirtz, S. (1973) *Patterns in the Early Poetry of Israel*, Studies in Ancient Oriental Civilization 32, 2nd edition, Chicago: University of Chicago Press.

Globe, A. (1974) "The Literary Structure and Unity of the Song of Deborah," *JBL* 93:493–512.

—— (1990) "'Enemies Round About': Disintegrative Structure in the Book of Judges," in V.L Tollers and J. Maier (eds) *Mapping of the Biblical Terrain: The Bible as Text,* Bucknell Review, Lewisburg: Bucknell University Press.

Gooding, D.W. (1982) "The Composition of the Book of Judges," *ErIsr* 16:70*–79*.

Goodwin, D.W. (1969) *Text-Restoration Methods in Contemporary U.S.A. Biblical Scholarship*, Naples: Isituto Orientale di Napoli.

Gordon, R.P. (1995) "A House Divided: Wisdom in Old Testament Narrative Traditions," in J. Day *et al.* (eds) *Wisdom in Ancient Israel: Essays in Honour of J. A. Emerton*, Cambridge: Cambridge University Press.

Gottlieb, I.B. (1991) "*Sof Davar*: Biblical Endings," *Prooftexts* 11:214–15.

Grabbe, L.L. (ed.) (1997) *Can A 'History of Israel' Be Written?* JSOTSup 245, Sheffield: Sheffield Academic Press.

Gray, J. (1977) "A Cantata of the Autumn Festival:Psalm LXVIII," *JSS* 22:2–26.

—— (1988) "Israel in the Song of Deborah," in L. Eslinger and G. Taylor (eds) *Ascribe to the LORD: Biblical and Other Studies in Memory of Peter C. Craigie*, JSOTSup 67, Sheffield: Sheffield Academic Press.

Greenblatt, S.J. (1988) *Shakespearean Negotiations: The Circulation of Social Energy in Renaissance England*, Berkeley: University of California Press.

Greenspahn, F.E. (1986) "The Theology of the Framework of Judges," *VT* 36:385–96.

Guest, P.D. (1998) "Can Judges Survive without Sources? Challenging the Consensus," *JSOT* 78:43–61.

Gunkel, H. (1994) *The Stories of Genesis*, Vallejo, CA: Bibal.

Gunkel, H. and Begrich, J. (1966) *Einleitung in die Psalmen: Die Gattungen der religiösen Lyrik Israels*, 2nd edition, Göttingen: Vandenhoeck & Ruprecht.

Gunn, D.M. (1980) *The Fate of King Saul: An Interpretation of a Biblical Story*, JSOTSup 14, Sheffield: JSOT Press.

—— (1987) "New Directions in the Study of Biblical Hebrew Narrative," *JSOT* 39:65–75.

Hackett, J.A. (1987) "Women's Studies and the Hebrew Bible," in R.E. Friedman and H.G.M. Williamson (eds) *The Future of Biblical Studies: The Hebrew Scriptures*, Semeia Studies, Atlanta: Scholars.

—— (1998) "'There Was No King in Israel': The Era of the Judges," in M.D. Coogan (ed.) *The Oxford History of the Biblical World*, New York: Oxford University Press.

Hahn, H.F. (1966) *The Old Testament in Modern Research*, Philadelphia: Fortress.

Halpern, B. (1983a) "Doctrine by Misadventure: Between the Israelite Source and the Biblical Historian," in R.E. Friedman (ed.) *The Poet and the Historian: Essays in Literary and Historical Biblical Criticism*, HSS 26, Chico, CA: Scholars.

—— (1983b) "The Resourceful Israelite Historian: The Song of Deborah and Israelite Historiography," *HTR* 76:379–401.

—— (1988) *The First Historians: The Hebrew Bible and History*, San Francisco: Harper & Row.

Haskell, T.L. (1998) *Objectivity is Not Neutrality: Explanatory Schemes in History*, Baltimore: Johns Hopkins University Press.

Hauser, A.J. (1980) "Judges 5: Parataxis in Hebrew Poetry," *JBL* 99:23–41.

—— (1987) "Two Songs of Victory: A Comparison of Exodus 15 and Judges 5," in E.R. Follis (ed.) *Directions in Biblical Hebrew Poetry*, JSOTSup 40, Sheffield: JSOT Press.

Hendel, R.S. (1987) "Of Demigods and the Deluge: Toward an Interpretation of Genesis 6:1–4," *JBL* 106:13–26.

Hobsbawm, E. and Ranger, T. (eds) (1983) *The Invention of Tradition*, Cambridge: Cambridge University Press.

Houston, W.J. (1997) "Misunderstanding or Midrash? The Prose Appropriation of Poetic Material in the Hebrew Bible," *ZAW* 109:342–55, 534–48.

Hudson, D.M. (1994) "Living in a Land of Epithets: Anonymity in Judges 19–21," *JSOT* 62:49–66.

Huizinga, J. (1975) "A Definition of the Concept of History," in R. Klibansky and H.J. Paton (eds) *Philosophy and History: Essays Presented to Ernst Cassirer*, Gloucester, MA: Peter Smith.

Iggers, G. (1997) *Historiography in the Twentieth Century: From Scientific Objectivity to the Postmodern Challenge*, Hanover: Wesleyan University Press.

Jemielty, T. (1992) *Satire and the Hebrew Prophet*, Louisville, KY: Westminster/John Knox.

Jones, B.W. (1977) "Two Misconceptions about the Book of Esther," *CBQ* 39:171–81.

Jones-Warsaw, K. (1993) "Toward a Womanist Hermeneutic: A Reading of Judges 19–21," in A. Brenner (ed.) *A Feminist Companion to Judges*, Feminist Companion to the Bible 4, Sheffield: JSOT Press.

Josephus, F. (1968) *Jewish Antiquities, Books V–VIII*, trans. H.St.J. Thackery, Loeb Classics, Cambridge: Harvard University Press.

Joyce, P. (1994) "First Among Equals?: The Historical-Critical Approach in the Marketplace of Methods," in S. Porter *et al.* (eds) *Crossing the Boundaries: Essays in Biblical Interpretation in Honour of Michael D. Goulder*, Biblical Interpretation Series 8, Leiden: Brill.

Jull, T.A. (1988) "מקרה in Judges 3: A Scatological Reading," *JSOT* 81:63–75.

Jüngling, H.-W. (1981) *Richter 19 – Ein Plädoyer für das Königtum: Stilistische Analyse der Tendenzerzählung Ri 19,1–30a; 21,25*, AnBib 84, Rome: Biblical Institute Press.

Kalimi, I. (2000) *The Book of Chronicles: Historical Writing and Literary Devices*, The Biblical Encyclopedia Library 18, Jerusalem: Mosad Bialik (Hebrew) (Published in German as [1995] *Zur Geschichtsschreibung des Chronisten*, BZAW 226, Berlin: de Gruyter).

Kamuf, P. (1993) "Author of a Crime," in A. Brenner (ed.) *A Feminist Companion to Judges*, Feminist Companion to the Bible 4, Sheffield: JSOT Press.

Kantra, R.A (1984) *All Things Vain: Religious Satirists and Their Art*, University Park, PA: Pennsylvania State University Press.

Klaus, N. (1999) *Pivot Patterns in the Former Prophets*, JSOTSup 247, Sheffield: Sheffield Academic Press.

Klein, L.R. (1993) "The Book of Judges: Paradigm and Deviation in Images of Women," in A. Brenner (ed.) *A Feminist Companion to Judges*, Feminist Companion to the Bible 4, Sheffield: JSOT Press.

Koch, K. (1969) *The Growth of the Biblical Tradition: The Form-Critical Method*, London: Adam and Charles Black.

Kraus, H.-J. (1988) *Psalms 1–59*, trans. H.C. Oswald, Minneapolis: Augsburg.

Kravitz, K.F. (1999) *Divine Trophies of War in Assyria and Ancient Israel: Case Studies in Political Theology*, unpublished Ph.D. Dissertation, Brandeis University.

Kugel, J. (1981a) *The Idea of Biblical Poetry: Parallelism and Its History*, New Haven, CT: Yale University Press.

—— (1981b) "On the Bible and Literary Criticism," *Prooftexts* 1:217–36.

—— (1982) "James Kugel Responds," *Prooftexts* 2:328–32.

Kuntz, J.K. (1992) "Kenaz," *ABD* 4:17.

Kutscher, E.Y. (1982) *A History of the Hebrew Language*, Jerusalem: Magnes.

Landy, F. (1984) "Poetics and Parallelism: Some Comments on James Kugel's *The Idea of Biblical Poetry*," *JSOT* 28:61–87.

Lasine, S. (1984) "Guest and Host in Judges 19: Lot's Hospitality in an Inverted World," *JSOT* 29:37–59.

Lemche, N.P. (1983) "The Judges – Once More," *BN* 20:47–55.

—— (1985) *Early Israel:Anthropological and Historical Studies on the Israelite Society Before the Monarchy*, VTSup 37, Leiden: Brill.

—— (1998) *The Israelites in History and Tradition*, London: SPCK.

Levinson, B.M. (1991) *The Hermeneutics of Innovation: The Impact of Centralization Upon the Structure, Sequence, and Reformulation of Legal Material in Deuteronomy*, unpublished Ph.D. Dissertation, Brandeis University.

—— (1997) *Deuteronomy and the Hermeneutics of Legal Innovation*, New York: Oxford University Press.

Lindars, B. (1995) *Judges 1–5: A New Translation and Commentary*, Edinburgh: T & T Clark.

Long, B. (1991) "The 'New' Biblical Poetics of Alter and Sternberg," *JSOT* 51:71–84.

Longman III, T. (1987) *Literary Approaches to Biblical Interpretation*, Grand Rapids, MI: Zondervan.

—— (1991) *Fictional Akkadian Autobiography: A Generic and Comparative Study*, Winona Lake, IN: Eisenbrauns.

McCarter, Jr., P.K. (1980) *I Samuel*, AB 8, Garden City, NY: Doubleday.

—— (1984) *II Samuel*, AB 9, Garden City, NY: Doubleday.

McKenzie, S.L. (1992) "The Deuteronomistic History," *ABD* 2:161–8.

McKenzie, S.L. and Graham, M.P. (1994) *The History of Israel's Traditions: The Heritage of Martin Noth*, JSOTSup 182, Sheffield: Sheffield Academic Press.

Madsen, D.L. (1994) *Rereading Allegory: A Narrative Approach to Genre*, New York: St. Martins.

Magonet, J. (1976) *Form and Meaning: Studies in Literary Techniques in the Book of Jonah*, BBET 2, Bern: Herbert Land.

—— (1992) "Jonah, Book of," *ABD* 3:937–8.

Malamat, A. (1954) "Cushan Rishathaim and the Decline of the Near East Around 1200 B.C.," *JNES* 13: 231–42.

Margalith, O. (1985) "Samson's Foxes," *VT* 35:224–9.

—— (1986a) "More Samson Legends," *VT* 36:397–405.

—— (1986b) "Samson's Riddles and Samson's Magical Locks," *VT* 36:225–34.

—— (1987) "The Legends of Samson/Heracles," *VT* 37:63–70.

Martineau, W.H. (1972) "A Model of the Social Function of Humor," in J.H. Goldstein and P.E. McGhee (eds) *The Psychology of Humor: Theoretical Perspectives and Empirical Issues*, New York: Academic Press.

Matthews, V.H. (1992) "Hospitality and Hostility in Genesis 19 and Judges 19," *BTB* 22:3–11.

Mayes, A.D.H. (1969) "The Historical Context of the Battle Against Sisera," *VT* 19:353–60.

Milgrom, J. (1982) "Religious Conversion and the Revolt Model for the Formation of Israel," *JBL* 101:169–76.

—— (1990) *Numbers*, JPS Torah Commentary 4, Philadelphia: Jewish Publication Society.

Miller, G.P. (1996) "Verbal Feud in the Hebrew Bible: Judges 3:12–30 and 19–21," *JNES* 55:114–15.

—— (1998) "A Riposte Form in the Song of Deborah," in V.H. Matthews *et al.* (eds) *Gender and Law in the Hebrew Bible and the Ancient Near East*, JSOTSup 262, Sheffield: Sheffield Academic Press.

Miller, J.M. and Hayes, J.H. (1986) *A History of Ancient Israel and Judah*, Philadelphia: Westminster.

Miller, Jr., P.D. and Roberts, J.J.M. (1977) *The Hand of the Lord: A Reassessment of the "Ark Narrative" of 1 Samuel*, Baltimore: Johns Hopkins University Press.

Minor, M. (1992) *Literary–Critical Approaches to the Bible: An Annotated Bibliography*, West Cornwall, CT: Locust Hill.

Miscall, P.D. (1986) *1 Samuel: A Literary Reading*, Bloomington: Indiana University Press.

Moles, J.L. (1993) "Truth and Untruth in Herodotus and Thucydides," in C. Gill and T.P. Wiseman (eds) *Lies and Fiction in the Ancient World*, Austin: University of Texas Press.

Moore, G.F. (1895) *Judges*, ICC 7, Edinburgh: T & T Clark.

Muilenburg, J. (1969) "Form Criticism and Beyond," *JBL* 88:1–18.

Mullen, Jr., E.T. (1982) "The 'Minor Judges': Some Literary and Historical Considerations," *CBQ* 44:185–201.

—— (1984) "Judges 1:1–3:6: The Deuteronomistic Reintroduction of the Book of Judges," *HTR* 77:33–64.

Müllner, I. (1999) "Lethal Differences: Sexual Violence as Violence Against Others in Judges 19," in A. Brenner (ed.) *Judges: A Feminist Companion to the Bible*, Feminist Companion to the Bible, Second Series, 4, Sheffield: Sheffield Academic Press.

Murphy, R.E. (1992) "Wisdom in the OT," *ABD* 6:920–31.

Na'aman, N. (1994) "The 'Conquest of Canaan' in the Book of Joshua and in History," in I. Finkelstein and N. Na'aman (eds) *From Nomadism to Monarchy: Archaeological and Historical Aspects of Early Israel*, Jerusalem: Israel Exporation Society.

Newsom, C.A. (1989) "Woman and the Discourse of Patriarchal Wisdom: A Study of Proverbs 1–9," in P.L. Day (ed.) *Gender and Difference in Ancient Israel*, Minneapolis: Fortress.

Nicholson, E. (1998) *The Pentateuch in the Twentieth Century: The Legacy of Julius Wellhausen*, Oxford: Clarendon.

Niditch, S. (1982) "The 'Sodomite' Theme in Judges 19–21:Family, Community, and Social Disintegration," *CBQ* 44:35–78.

—— (1990) "Samson as Culture Hero, Trickster, and Bandit: The Empowerment of the Weak," *CBQ* 52:608–24.

Noble, P.R. (1993) "Synchronic and Diachronic Approaches to Biblical Interpretation," *Journal of Literature and Theology* 7:130–48.

—— (1996) "A 'Balanced' Reading of the Rape of Dinah: Some Exegetical and Methodological Observations," *BibInt* 4:173–204.

Noth, M. (1960) *The History of Israel*, 2nd edition, New York: Harper & Row.

—— (1981) *The Deuteronomistic History*, JSOTSup 15, Sheffield: JSOT Press.

Novick, P. (1988) *That Noble Dream: The "Objectivity Question" and the American Historical Profession*, Cambridge: Cambridge University Press.

O'Connell, R.H. (1996) *The Rhetoric of the Book of Judges*, VTSup 63, Leiden: Brill.

O'Connor, M, (1986) "The Women in the Book of Judges," *HAR* 10:277–93.

O'Doherty, E. (1956) "The Literary Problem of Judges 1,1–3,6," *CBQ* 18:3–4.

Penchansky, D. (1992) "Staying the Night: Intertextuality in Genesis and Judges," in D.N. Fewell (ed.) *Reading Between Texts: Intertextuality and the Hebrew Bible*, Louisville, KY: Westminster/John Knox.

Polzin R. (1989) *Samuel and the Deuteronomist: A Literary Study of the Deuteronomistic History, Part Two: 1 Samuel*, San Francisco: Harper & Row.

Porter, B.N. (1993) *Images, Power, and Politics: Figurative Aspects of Esarhaddon's Babylonian Policy*, Philadelphia: American Philosophical Society.

Pritchard, J.B. (ed.) (1955) *Ancient Near Eastern Texts Relating to the Old Testament*, 2nd edition, Princeton: Princeton University Press.

Radday, Y.T. and Brenner, A. (1990) *On Humour and the Comic in the Hebrew Bible*, JSOTSup 92, Sheffield: Sheffield Academic Press.

Rehm, M.D. (1992) "Levites and Priests," *ABD* 4:297–310.

Reinhartz, A. (1992) "Samson's Mother: An Unnamed Protagonist," *JSOT* 55:25–37 (reprinted in [1993] A. Brenner [ed.] *A Feminist Companion to Judges*, Feminist Companion to the Bible 4, Sheffield: Sheffield Academic Press).

—— (1998) *"Why Ask my Name?" Anonymity and Identity in Biblical Narrative*, New York: Oxford University Press.

Rendtorff, R. (1993) "The Paradigm is Changing: Hopes – And Fears," *BibInt* 1:34–53.

Richter, W. (1963) *Traditionsgeschichtliche Untersuchungen zum Richterbuch*, BBB 18, Bonn: Peter Hanstein.

—— (1964) *Die Bearbeitungen des "Retterbuches" in der Deuteronomischen Epoche*, BBB 21, Bonn: Peter Hanstein.

—— (1966) "Die Überlieferungen um Jephtah:Ri 10,17–12,6," *Bib* 47:485–556.

Robertson, D.A. (1972) *Linguistic Evidence in Dating Early Hebrew Poetry*, Missoula, MT: Society of Biblical Literature.

Rofé, A. (1985) "The Laws of Warfare in the Book of Deuteronomy: Their Origins, Intent and Positivity," *JSOT* 32:23–44.

—— (1988) *The Prophetical Stories*, Jerusalem: Magnes.

Römer, T.C. (1998) "Why Would the Deuteronomist Tell About the Sacrifice of Jephthah's Daughter?" *JSOT* 72:27–38.

Rosenheim, E.R. (1971) "The Satiric Spectrum," in R. Paulson (ed.) *Satire: Modern Essays in Criticism*, Prentice-Hall English Literature Series, Englewood Cliffs, NJ: Prentice Hall.

Rosenthal, F. (1956) *Humor in Early Islam*, Philadelphia: University of Pennsylvania Press.

Rudman, D. (1997) "Woman as Divine Agent in Ecclesiastes," *JBL* 116:411–27.

Sasson, J.M. (1990) *Jonah*, AB 24b, New York: Doubleday.

Schloen, J.D. (1993) "Caravans, Kenites and *Casus belli*: Enmity and Alliance in the Song of Deborah," *CBQ* 55:18–38.

Schneider, T.J. (2000) *Judges*, Berit Olam, Collegeville, MN: Liturgical.

Scholes, R. (1981) "Afterthoughts on Narrative: Language, Narrative, and Anti-Narrative," in W.J.T. Mitchell (ed.) *On Narrative*, Chicago: University of Chicago Press.

Seeligmann, I.L. (1963) "Menschliches Heldentum und göttlich Hilfe: Die doppente Kausalität im alttestamentlichen Geschichtsdenken," *TZ* 19:385–411.

Simon, U. (1999) *Jonah*, JPS Bible Commentary, Philadelphia: Jewish Publication Society.

Smend, R. (1971) "Das Gesetz und die Völker: Ein Beitrag zur deuteronomistischen Redaktionsgeschichte," in H.W. Wolff (ed.) *Problemer biblischer Theologie: Gerhard von Rad zum 70. Geburthstag*, Munich: Chr. Kaiser.

Smith, B.H. (1968) *Poetic Closure*, Chicago: University of Chicago Press.

Soggin, J.A. (1981) *Judges*, OTL, Philadelphia: Westminster.

—— (1984) *A History of Ancient Israel*, Philadelphia: Westminster.

Sommer, B.D. (1998) *A Prophet Reads Scripture: Allusion in Isaiah 40–66*, Stanford: Stanford University Press.

Speiser, E.A. (1964) *Genesis*, AB 1, Garden City, NY: Doubleday.

Stager, L.E. (1986) "Archaeology, Ecology, and Social History: Background Themes to the Song of Deborah," in J. Emerton (ed.) *Jerusalem Congress Volume*, VTSup 40, Leiden: Brill.

—— (1989) "The Song of Deborah: Why Some Tribes Answered the Call and Others Did Not," *BAR* 15/1:51–64.

Sternberg, M. (1985) *The Poetics of Biblical Narrative: Ideological Literature and the Drama of Reading*, Bloomington: Indiana University Press.

—— (1992) "Biblical Poetic and Sexual Politics: From Reading to Counter-Reading," *JBL* 111:463–88.

Stone, K. (1995) "Gender and Homosexuality in Judges 19: Subject-Honor, Object-Shame?" *JSOT* 67:87–107.

Stone, L.G. (1988) *From Tribal Confederation to Monarchic State: The Editorial Perspective of the Book of Judges*, unpublished Ph.D. Dissertation, Yale University.

Sweeney, A. (1997) "Davidic Polemic in the Book of Judges," *VT* 47: 517–29.

Talmon, S. (1963) "'Wisdom' in the Book of Esther," *VT* 13:419–55.

—— (1978) "The Presentation of Synchroneity and Simultaneity in Biblical Narrative," *ScrHier* 27:9–26.

Talstra, E. (1993) *Solomon's Prayer: Synchrony and Diachrony in the Composition of I Kings 8, 14–61*, Kampen: Kok.

—— (1998) "From the 'Eclipse' to the 'Art' of Biblical Narrative: Reflections on Methods of Biblical Exegesis," in F. García Martínez and E. Noort (eds) *Perspectives in the Study of the Old Testament and Early Judaism: A Symposium in Honour of Adams S. van der Woude on the Occasion of His 70th Birthday*, VTSup 73, Leiden: Brill.

Thompson, T.L. (1974) *The Historicity of the Patriarchal Narratives*, BZAW 133, Berlin: Walter de Gruyter.

—— (1992) *Early History of the Israelite People From the Written and Archaeological Sources*, SHANE 4, Leiden: Brill.

—— (1999) *The Mythic Past: Biblical Archaeology and the Myth of Israel*, New York: Basic Books.

Todorov, T. (1976) "The Origin of Genres," *NLH* 8:159–70.

Trible, P. (1984) *Texts of Terror: Literary=Feminist Readings of Biblical Narratives*, Philadelphia:Fortress.

—— (1994) *Rhetorical Criticism:Context, Method, and the Book of Jonah*, Guides to Biblical Scholarship, Minneapolis:Fortress.

Tsevat, M. (1980) *The Meaning of the Book of Job and Other Biblical Studies: Essays on the Literature and Religion of the Hebrew Bible*, New York: Ktav.

—— (1992) "Was Samson a Nazirite?" in M. Fishbane and E. Tov (eds) *"Sha'arei Talmon": Studies in the Bible, Qumran, and the Ancient Near East Presented to Shemaryahu Talmon*, Winona Lake, IN: Eisenbrauns.

Unterman, J. (1980) "The Literary Influence of 'The Binding of Isaac' (Genesis 22) on 'The Outrage at Gibeah' (Judges 19)," *HAR* 4: 161–5.

van der Kooij, A. (1996) "On Male and Female Views in Judges 4 and 5," in B. Becking and M. Dijkstra (eds) *On Reading Prophetic Texts: Gender-Specific and Related Studies in Memory of Fokkelien van Dijk-Hemmes*, Biblical Interpretation Series 18, Leiden:Brill.

van Seters, J. (1975a) *Abraham in History and Tradition*, New Haven, CT:Yale University Press.

—— (1975b) *In Search of History: Historiography in the Ancient World and the Origins of Biblical History*, New Haven, CT: Yale University Press.

van Wolde, E. (1996) "Deborah and Ya'el in Judges 4," in B. Becking and M. Dijkstra (eds) *On Reading Prophetic Texts: Gender-Specific and Related Studies in Memory of Fokkelien van Dijk-Hemmes*, Biblical Interpretation Series 18, Leiden:Brill.

von Rad, G. (1972) *Wisdom in Israel*, London:SCM.

—— (1976) "The Joseph Narrative and Ancient Wisdom," in J.L. Crenshaw (ed.) *Studies in Ancient Israelite Wisdom*, New York:Ktav.

Waltisberg, M. (1999) "Zum Alter der Sprache des Deboraliedes Ri 5," *ZAH* 12:218–32.

Watson, W.G.E. (1986) *Classical Hebrew Poetry: A Guide to Its Techniques*, JSOTSup 26, Sheffield: JSOT Press.

Watts, J.W. (1992) *Psalm and Story: Inset Hymns in Hebrew Narrative*, JSOTSup 139, Sheffield: Sheffield Academic Press.

Webb, B. (1987) *The Book of Judges: An Integrated Reading*, JSOTSup 46, Sheffield: JSOT Press.

Weinfeld, M. (1967) "The Period of the Conquest and the Judges as Seen by the Earlier and the Later Sources," *VT* 17:93–113.

—— (1993) "Judges 1.1–1:5:The Conquest under the Leadership of the House of Judah," in A.G. Auld (ed.) *Understanding Poets and Prophets: Essays in Honour of George Wishart Anderson*, JSOTSup 152, Sheffield: Sheffield Academic Press.

Weiser, A. (1959) "Das Deboralied: Eine gattungs – und traditions – geschichtliche Studien," *ZAW* 71:67–97.

Weisman, Z. (1998) *Political Satire in the Bible*, SBL Semeia Studies 32, Atlanta: Scholars.

Weitzman, S. (1997) *Song and Story in Biblical Narrative: The History of a Literary Convention in Ancient Israel*, Bloomington, IN: Indiana University Press.

Wellhausen, J. (1973) *Prolegomena to the History of Ancient Israel, with a Reprint of the Article* 'Israel' *from the Encyclopedia Britannica*, Gloucester, MA: Peter Smith.

Wharton, J.A. (1973) "The Secret of Yahweh: Story and Affirmation in Judges 13–16." *Int* 27:48–66.

Wilson, E.O. (2000) *Sociobiology, the New Synthesis: The Twenty-fifth Anniversary Edition*, Cambridge, MA: Harvard University Press.

Wilson, R.R. (1977) *Genealogy and History in the Biblical World*, YNER 7, New Haven, CT: Yale University Press.

—— (1992) "Genealogy, Genealogies," *ABD* 2:929–32.

Wiseman, T.P. (1993) "Lying Historians: Seven Types of Mendacity," in C. Gill and T.P. Wiseman (eds) *Lies and Fiction in the Ancient World*, Austin: University of Texas Press.

Wright, G.E. (1946) "The Literary and Historical Problem of Joshua 10 and Judges 1," *JNES* 5:105–14.

Yee, G.A. (1995) "Ideological Criticism: Judges 17–21 and the Dismembered Body," in G.A. Yee (ed.) *Judges and Method: New Approaches in Biblical Studies*, Minneapolis: Fortress.

Yellin, D. (1934) *Gan Hammeshalim We-Hahidoth: Diwan of Don Tadros Son of Abu–'el–'äfiah*, 2/1, Jerusalem: Weiss.

Younger, Jr., K.L. (1991) "Heads! Tails! Or the Whole Coin?! Contextual Method & Intertextual Analysis: Judges 4 and 5," in K.L. Younger *et al.* (eds) *The Biblical Canon in Comparative Perspective: Scripture in Context IV*, Lewiston: Edwin Mellen.

—— (1994) "Judges 1 in Its Near Eastern Literary Context," in A.R. Millard (ed.) *Faith, Tradition, and History: Old Testament Historiography in Its Near Eastern Context*, Winona Lake, IN: Eisenbrauns.

Zakovitch, Y. (1978) *The Pattern of the Numerical Sequence Three-Four in the Bible*, unpublished Ph.D. Dissertation, Hebrew University.

—— (1982) *The Life of Samson (Judges 13–16): A Critical-Literary Analysis*, Jerusalem: Magnes (Hebrew).

—— (1983) "The Associative Arrangement of the Book of Judges and Its Use for the Recognition of Stages in the Formation of the Book," in Y. Zakovitch and A. Rofé (eds), *The Isac Leo Seeligmann Volume*, Jerusalem: Rubenstein.

GENERAL INDEX

Abigail 13
allegory 27–28
allusion 75, 85–8, 88–9, see also inner–biblical interpretation; verbal allusion
Annunciation story 43, 45
anthropological approach 83
anti–Saul polemic 88, 113, 115
appendices, Book of Jeremiah 81; Judges see Judges, Book of, appendix; Samuel, Book of, 81, 94, 113
Aramaisms 65
archaeology 3, 6, 63, 64
archaic biblical poetry 61, 62–4
associative ordering 109–10

Barak 24
barren woman motif 45
Benjamin(ites) 81, 88, 89, 90, 98, 101, 111
Bible as literature see literary approaches; literature
biblical chronology 3

Caleb 2, 26, 31, 100
canonical criticism 62
canonization 49
catch–lines see associative ordering
chiasm 11, 12, 105, 118 see also literary devices
chronicler 78
Chronicles, Book of 19, 78, 96, 118, 120
chronological ordering of stories 60, 61, 109, 119
comparative approach 77
Concubine 80–2, 86, 90, 91
conquest 3, 26, 92, 93, 96, 98, 100, 101, 102, 109, 110
contradiction as evidence of compositeness 41, 93, 96, 97, 100
Copenhagen School ix, 6, 20, 117
Cushan–rishathaim 4, 26, 27

Dagon 57–8
Daniel, Book of ix
Danites 80
dating of biblical texts 3, 12, 16, 32, 48, 61–65, 89
David 12, 13, 15, 18, 25, 33, 89, 98, 100, 110–16
Dead Sea Scrolls 41, 44, 96
Deborah 24, 39, 61–79, 112
deconstructionism 7
Delilah episode 55–6, 58, 59, 81, 82
Deuteronomistic History (DtrH) 25, 26, 40, 42, 75, 76, 78, 83, 98, 103, 106, 114, 119
Deuteronomy, Book of 40, 95
diachronic analysis 10, 14, 15, 18, 19
double entendre 45
double traditions as emphasis 113; as historical method 78
duplication as evidence of compositeness 41 see also parallel episodes

Ecclesiastes, Book of see Qohelet, Book of
editorial devices 55, 95, 110, 113 see also chronological ordering of stories; double traditions as emphasis; inclusio; inner–biblical interpretation; resumptive repetitions; verbal allusions
Egypt 4, 77; New Kingdom 16
Ehud x, 6, 22, 23, 24, 28–38, 39, 42, 106, 111, 112, 119
ending formula 42, 54, 81
Enuma Elish 14
Ephraim(ites) 80, 90, 101, 112, 113
Epic of Gilgamesh 16
Esther, Book of ix, 89, 119
etiology 25, 54, 55, 107
events 1, 3, 5, 7, 30
exilic period 32, 112, 115, 121
external evidence 3, 5, 65, 96
Ezra–Nehemiah, Book of 2, 96

137

SCRIPTURE INDEX